HAUNTED
STOCKTON

HAUNTED STOCKTON

Robert Woodhouse

The
History
Press

First published 2011

The History Press
The Mill, Brimscombe Port
Stroud, Gloucestershire, GL5 2QG
www.thehistorypress.co.uk

British Library Cataloguing in Publication Data.
A catalogue record for this book is available from the British Library.

ISBN 978 0 7524 5763 5
Typesetting and origination by The History Press
Printed in Great Britain

Contents

Acknowledgements

A lifetime's interest in the history of north-east England, and the Teesside area in particu-lar, has provided numerous reports of supernatural activity. Many of these incidents were highlighted in local newspapers, almanacs and assorted reference works, but others have been recalled first hand by friends, relatives and members of the public and I am grateful to all the individuals and organisations who have provided such material.

Locations covered are now within Stockton-on-Tees District Council. In particular I am indebted to staff at Stockton-on-Tees Reference Library for their assistance in trac-ing material in newspapers and various reference works and to members of my classes on 'Supernatural North Country' for unearthing additional features. Wardens and staff at Preston Hall, Elmwood Youth and Community Centre, and Kiora Hall have also supplied useful information. A final word of thanks is due to Sandra Mylan for her typing and administrative work.

Introduction

Few topics of conversation arouse quite as much debate as the subject of hauntings. Some folk remain distinctly sceptical while others recall dramatic supernatural stories in chillingly clear detail, and an increased interest in ghostly sightings is reflected in the number and frequency of groups making on-site investigations.

Northerners, it seems, are at the forefront when it comes to ghostly credentials; a recent National Opinion Poll found that six out of ten people in the region claimed to have felt the presence of a ghost. This figure far outweighed numbers calculated for the Midlands and south of England. These regional differences are, perhaps, put down to willingness on the part of northerners to be open and honest about supernatural sightings.

It must be no surprise that most reported spectral sightings are linked to locations with a long history of human occupation and in the northern area these include York, Manchester, Newcastle-on-Tyne and Durham. Stockton's position as a trading centre and its importance as a base for successive Bishops of Durham with their retainers brought any number of colourful local and visiting characters.

Down the centuries ghostly characters and paranormal themes have regularly featured in literary works, but the whole question of ghosts, phantoms, apparitions (or whatever term is applied) only started to gain widespread publicity in Britain during the seventeenth century. This groundswell of interest was due, at least in part, to an increase in witchcraft. In more recent times the subject of ghost hunting has gained academic credibility and committed groups of researchers now employ a range of technical devices during their investigations. Scientific analysis of reported supernatural sightings has produced data to explain how a ghost is created and material to expose fake reports, along with interpretations of the episode.

If spectral sightings are linked to events or incidents connected with the full range of human activity in the past, then the area covered by the modern-day Stockton-on-Tees Borough Council has an impressive range of settings – both urban and rural – within its boundaries.

Since the 1980s excavations at Norton have unearthed a fascinating sequence of cemeteries. The earliest burials dated from the period AD 550–610, before the arrival of Christianity, and later adjacent cemeteries – moving in an east-west direction, towards St Mary's Church – indicate a sizeable local population following the arrival of Christian practices.

Stockton's importance as a river crossing point on a strategic north-south route and its growth as a market centre during the medieval period brought a range of traders and craft-workers to the township. The presence of the Bishop of Durham's riverside manor house provided a stream of eminent visitors, including royalty and nobility, before Stockton and neighbouring Yarm were embroiled in military action during the English Civil War.

An improved road network and the advent of the coaching era saw the emergence of coaching taverns and inns at stopping places such as Yarm and Stockton where racecourses, theatres and blood sports such as bear-baiting and cock-fighting added a raucous edge to the urban scene. The arrival of the pressgang on Stockton's river frontage brought further disruption to the township during the early nineteenth century, and the arrival of the Stockton and Darlington Railway in 1825 heralded a rapid phase of industrialisation in the Stockton area.

As shipyards and a host of industries ranging from small scale potteries to massive iron making enterprises spread along the riverbanks areas of tightly packed terraced housing were completed for workers and their families. During the last century, housing developments in suburban areas have linked outlying settlements such as Hartburn and Eaglescliffe to central Stockton and though outlying sectors on the rural fringe have seen little alteration, town centres at Stockton, Thornaby and Billingham have seen huge changes.

Yarm's High Street retains much of its earlier character and style but phases of redevelopment have radically altered other urban centres. Yet it could well be that the assortment of supernatural phenomena provide an intriguing link with earlier times in the Stockton area.

Robert Woodhouse, 2011

A Brief History of Stockton-on-Tees

Setting the Spooky Scene

Before we venture into the accounts of Stockton's various hauntings, perhaps one should be made aware of the foundations of rich history upon which they stand. Stockton's early importance in the realms of trade and commerce stemmed from port shipments (which first began in 1228) and a market which dates from 1310. The southern end of the settlement, however, was dominated by buildings which formed the Bishop of Durham's castle. Despite Stockton's early establishment of shipping and market trade, until the late 1600s, it was largely overshadowed by the nearby townships of Hartlepool, Darlington and Yarm, far bigger in size and importance in terms of their early commercial output than that of Stockton.

Market traders and visiting Bishops of Durham, with their assorted retinues, would certainly have brought an amount of colour and vitality to Stockton's High Street and riverside settings – but it was during the early eighteenth century that the town's fortunes changed dramatically.

In 1680, the customs house was moved from Hartlepool to Stockton when a large proportion of increased trade with London and the south was made up of butter shipments. Returning vessels brought goods

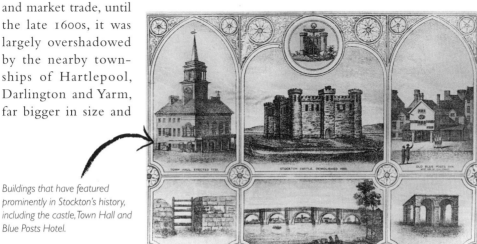

Buildings that have featured prominently in Stockton's history, including the castle, Town Hall and Blue Posts Hotel.

The parish church, with the rebuilt chancel of 1906, and the side chapel dating from 1925. The war memorial was erected in 1923.

an early 'ragged school' at his workshop in Finkle Street. He also drew up plans for 'cuts' in the course of the River Tees at Thornaby and Portrack, some forty years before the first of his schemes was carried out.

Thomas Sheraton was born in Stockton in 1751, where he received early schooling before taking up employment as a journeyman cabinet-maker. In about 1790, he moved to London and produced books on cabinet and furniture design before returning to Stockton as minister of the Baptist congregation in the early 1800s. He died on 22 October 1806 and it was some forty years before the significance of Sheraton's work was appreciated.

Stockton's best-known son is probably John Walker. Born on 29 May 1781 and raised in the High Street, he was educated in Durham and London before giving up a career as a surgeon to join a firm of druggists. During the early months of 1819, he set up a business at 59 High Street and, after years of experimentation with chemical compositions, he finally produced friction lights (matches) in 1826. John Walker moved to a property close to the parish church and in February 1858 he retired from business without patenting his invention. Following his death in May of the same year, he was buried in Norton churchyard.

A number of Stockton-born personalities made their way to the capital in order to pursue their careers. Brass Crosby moved to London, where he served as an attorney for a number of years before taking up office as councillor, sheriff and then alderman. On 29 September 1770, Crosby was elected Lord Mayor of London and soon became involved in a struggle with the House of Commons over press coverage of parliamentary proceedings. After a short period of imprisonment in the Tower of

such as rum, tobacco and tea, and with a growing demand for north-east coal, Stockton's riverside shipyards were soon building colliers for the east coast route.

Stockton remained a chapelry of Norton until 1711, when a fine red brick parish church was constructed at the northern end of the High Street. Further improvements followed in the shape of a townhouse (in 1735), a new roadway along the riverside from Finkle Street to Castlegate (during 1706) and between 1717 and 1720 central streets were cobbled.

In the early months of 1766, a barn in Green Dragon Yard was converted into the town's first theatre and the 1780s saw completion of a grammar school in West Row (1785) and the opening of buildings linked with the Blue Coat Charity School (1786).

With an increasing population and growth of the business and commercial sector came a number of eminent personalities. Edmund Harvey, a pewterer by trade, was born in the town in 1698 and set up

The northern end of the High Street, showing the parish church and cattle market (top right).

A group of workers at J.F. Smith & Co.'s Nebo Confectionery Works. The building served as a theatre from 1766 until the 1860s.

London he was released, in triumph, on 8 May 1771, with agreement that in future there would be no attempt to restrain publication of parliamentary debates.

Joseph Reed was born in March 1723 and combined an interest in writing dramatic poetry with running the family's rope-making business. In the late 1750s he moved his family and business interests to London, where his dramatic works enjoyed mixed fortunes.

In a similar vein, Joseph Ritson combined his work as conveyancer with an interest in regional verse and though he transferred business matters to London he made frequent visits to his hometown. During 1781 he issued 'The Stockton Jubilee or Shakespeare in all his Glory', a witty attack on local senior citizens, and following a visit to Paris, some tens years later, he gave firm backing to a Republican calendar.

A number of local men were drawn to a maritime career in times of commercial expansion and armed clashes with the Dutch and French navies. Numbered among these are Captain William Christopher and Captain Jonathan Fowler, as well as Christopher Allison, who distinguished himself as master of the *Adventurer* by capturing a French privateer in the English Channel, but perhaps most notable was Thomas Bertie.

Born in Stockton on 3 July 1758, Bertie began a long and illustrious career in the navy in October 1773. During his time onboard HMS *Seahorse*, he was a messmate of Nelson and Troubridge, and in 1777 he was promoted to the rank of lieutenant. Most of the next four years were spent aboard *The Monarch*, where he took part in several engagements against the French navy.

Further successes against French and Spanish fleets resulted in promotion to the rank of Rear Admiral of the Blue Squadron in 1808 and, although his health began to fail, Bertie enjoyed more success in the Baltic area. On 28 May 1825, he achieved the rank of Admiral but died some two weeks later.

Stockton earned a place in railway history with the formal opening of the line between Witton Park Colliery

In the early days of the railway, coaches were transferred from roads to bogeys on the rails – as with 'The Union'.

The Castle Theatre opened on 31 July 1908 and was re-named The Empire Theatre in 1912. After housing bingo sessions for a few years it was vacated in 1970 to make way for the Swallow Hotel.

and Stockton on 27 September 1825. *Locomotion No.1*'s arrival in Stockton was celebrated with a banquet in the Town Hall and the line is remembered as the first steam-worked public railway conveying traffic for reward.

During 1830, the line was extended eastwards from Stockton to 'Port Darlington' – as the new venture at Middlesbrough was known – and a rapid phase of industrial expansion got underway. Steam power was introduced for river and coastal trade and then sea-going vessels from the mid-nineteenth century, and at about the same time steam tramways were being constructed on local thoroughfares. On 22 October 1881 the Steam Tramway began operations from Brewery Bank, South Stockton (Thornaby) to Norton Green and the system continued in use until 31 December 1931.

The growing nineteenth-century township of Stockton provided a number of personalities who became household names in the entertainment world. William Thomson Hay was born at 23 Durham Street on 6 December 1888. His family soon left Stockton and moved to Lowestoft before returning to the North Country, and although Hay left school without taking examinations, he was soon carving out a career as a music hall star. A highly successful move into the world of movies saw him star in such films as *Oh, Mr Porter*, *Windbag the Sailor* and *The Black Sheep of Whitehall* – classics of the British cinema. Will Hay was also a firm favourite of the Royal Family.

Ivy Close was born in Stockton in 1890 and gained instant fame in 1908, when she won the *Daily Mirror* beauty contest.

Soon afterwards, she appeared in a week-long show at the town's Castle Theatre and by 1912 a career in films was underway. During 1916, Ivy began to make comedies for the famous Kalem Company in Florida, with many of her films directed by her husband Ronald Neame. Following his tragic death in 1923, she continued with character parts and completed a total of forty-four films between 1912 and 1929. Ivy died at Goring, Sussex on 4 December 1968 but her son, Ronald Neame, continued the family's connection with the film industry as a director.

The Stockton area produced a number of notable personalities in the music world but the best known of these was Doreen Stephens. Born in the town on 7 November 1922, she started singing at concerts and dances at the age of nine and,

five years later, she was spotted by another local born start of the entertainment world, Jimmy James.

Jack Hylton included her in his big band show and she appeared at the London Palladium at the age of fifteen. During the Second World War, Doreen entertained troops in a show that also featured Gracie Fields and Maurice Chevalier, and also performed with Maurice Winnick's band in Italy and the Middle East. From 1950, she spent twelve years with Billy Cotton and in two of her three Royal Command Performances with the band she was accompanied at the piano by her cousin, Bert Waller. After a long period of ill health, Doreen died in 1965 at the age of forty-two.

During the years between the First and Second World Wars, much of Stockton's housing had unfortunately become unfit for people to live in. Widespread clearance schemes in the late 1920s and early '30s included the riverside area of Thistle Green shopping premises along the High Street, which continued to draw large numbers of customers; there were claims that Stockton was one of the cheapest shopping centres in the North of England.

Post-war regeneration saw the completion of new estates at Ragworth, Fairfield, Newham Grange and Roseworth during the 1940s, while Stockton High Street was given a facelift during summer 1950, with the replacement of the wide cobbled surface with a dual carriageway. During the 1960s, Stockton gained a number of impressive buildings in the Church Road area. The Municipal Buildings were opened in 1961 at a cost of £200,000, the central library opened in March 1969 and on the opposite side of Church Road, the swimming baths and YMCA building were completed.

Stockton's days as a port ended on 23 August 1967, when a vessel named *Dora Reith* left Corporation Quay, and from the beginning of June 1970 work started on the £5 million redevelopment scheme of the High Street's east side.

HRH the Duke of Edinburgh visited Preston Park on 27 September 1975 for the 150th anniversary of the opening of the Stockton and Darlington Railway and ten years later the town celebrated three more notable anniversaries. Stockton market was 675 years old, the parish church marked 750 years of worship in the town, and the Town Hall celebrated 250 years of use.

Stockton gained a major arts venue with the opening of Arc in January 1999. Built on the site of the Dovecot Arts Centre and

The Regal Cinema opened on 22 April 1935 next to the Borough Hall at the southern end of the High Street.

Hippodrome-Essoldo cinema at a total cost of £11 million, the building included a theatre, a studio theatre, a cinema, flexible performance space, a digital studio and three bars. It suffered early operational difficulties and closed for fourteen months before re-opening in September 2003.

Work on the nearby £43 million Wellington Square shopping centre got underway on 13 March 2000, and celebrations to mark the official opening took place during October 2001, but it is the River Tees that has seen the most dramatic changes.

The Tees Barrage scheme reached a major landmark on 12 December 1994, when four 50-ton 'fish belly' gates were hoisted into position to halt sea water flowing upstream with the incoming tide. The official opening of the Tees Barrage complex took place on 18 July 1995, when HRH the Duke of Edinburgh performed the ceremony. A whole host of leisure activities including surfing, canoeing and sailing have since been developed on the twelve miles of tide-free water that extend upstream as far as Worsall.

In recent years, two more impressive bridges have been added to Stockton's skyline. Completed at a cost of £1.3 million, the Teesquay Millennium Footbridge was opened in December 2000 to link Stockton with the newly developed Teesdale site at Thornaby, and in May 2009 the graceful super structure of Infinity Bridge was officially opened.

Measuring 180 metres in length, it was fashioned from 450 tonnes of steel at a total cost of £15 million, and in May 2010 it won the International Association of Lighting Design Awards (IALDA) in Las Vegas, within days of winning a regional heat of the Royal Institute of British Architects Awards.

The working brief for Infinity Bridge was to design a symbolic structure to encourage members of the public to cross to the opposite riverbank and at the same time draw investors to develop available areas of riverside land (on the North Shore and Teesdale-Thornaby sites). As in earlier phases of Stockton's growth, the River Tees is again playing a crucial role in current regeneration, as well as providing cause for speculation as to the truth behind reported ghostly phenomena, as the next chapter explores. Read on, if you dare …

The Dodshon Memorial was unveiled on 26 August 1878 at a location on the High Street. It was later moved to Ropner Park (as shown here) before being returned, in recent years, to the High Street.

Market day scene, close to Dovecot Street (on the left).

A rather damp looking day on Stockton High Street.

17

The ornamental fountain and gardens at Ropner Park.

The Hippodrome, on the corner of Print Regent Street
and Dovecot Street, opened in 1905. It was then
renamed the Classic, then the Essoldo and finally the
Cannon, before its closure on 2 September 1993.

The Plaza Theatre in Bishop Street operated
from 1936 to 1959, after which it was used
for storage until this area was cleared in 1970.

Stockton's open-air theatre, built in 1951 to celebrate the Festival of Britain in Ropner Park.

The lake in Ropner Park. Land was donated by the Ropner family and the park was opened for public use on 4 October 1883 by the Duke and Duchess of York, later King George V and Queen Mary.

Upper section of former Altham's Tea Merchants premises – the only single-storey property on the High Street.

Properties in Brunswick Street erected in about 1820 and demolished in 1963.

Holy Trinity Vicarage in Yarm Lane. The vicarage was demolished in 1980.

St. John's Church with Nolan House and the gasworks in the background.

St John's Church was opened in 1874, closed in 1978 and demolished in 1980. An interesting feature was the building's Basilica-esque style.

Higher Grade School on Prince Regent Street.

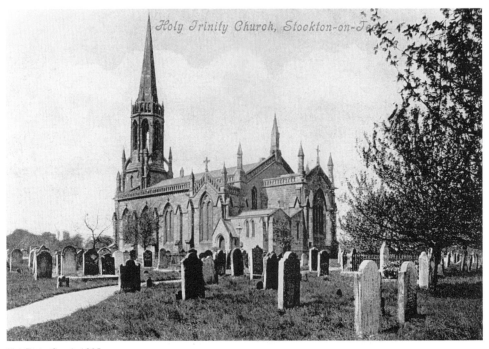

Holy Trinity Church, 1905.

Frontage of Brunswick Methodist Church in Dovecot Street. Opened in 1823, it was used for business premises before demolition.

Interior of Brunswick Methodist Chapel.

Methodist Chapel Sunday school at the rear of Brunswick Methodist Chapel.

Methodist Chapel Sunday School.

Business premises in the former Paradise Row Primitive Methodist Church on Church Road, which opened in 1866 and closed in 1945.

1
Spectral Images on the Tees

A Ghostly River Possessed?

In recent years, the waters of the River Tees have been kept under control and held in check by the impressive steelwork in the structure of the Tees Barrage. However, until now, this majestic northern river displayed a plethora of contrasting moods, in an anthropomorphic-like manner. Known to occasionally meander, and on other occasions surge aggressively around lowland bends, it was respected as a veritable force of nature, inspiring awe and invoking fear among many along its banks.

In 1771 and 1881, well-documented and destructive floods wreaked havoc for inhabitants living close to the river, and the fast-moving wall of water, known as the 'Tees Roll', has become part of local folklore, heightening the notion of a supernatural influence behind the aggressive waters. Yet even when the angry waters of the River Tees were seemingly kept secure in between the riverbanks, its headlong surge still met with trepidation and uneasiness amongst locals; feelings which still reign strong amongst locals today.

Victoria Bridge, linking Stockton and Thornaby, opened in 1887.

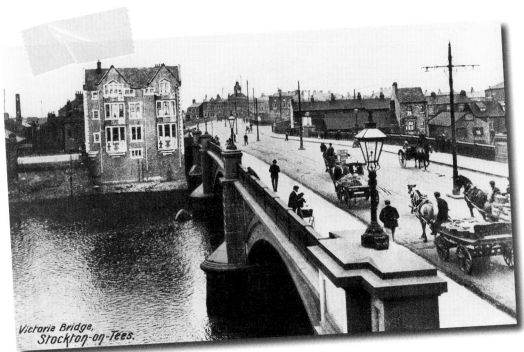

Victoria Bridge, Stockton-on-Tees.

Victoria Bridge and Bridge Hotel on the Thornaby bank.

Downstream view from Victoria Bridge.

Torrents of Scary Sounds and Freakish Formations

Following the aforementioned volatile river movements, an assortment of debris would be sent spinning, dipping, heaving or rearing downstream accompanied by a fearsome roar. The hours of darkness brought an air of mystery to this eerie and dramatic setting. It is little wonder then that the series of peculiar sounds and unnatural shapes led to reports of a ghostly hound on the banks of the Tees. Other northern rivers, ponds and lakes were said to be frequented by an evil spirit. Known as Jenny Greenteeth, this malevolent force would strike unexpectedly, dragging passers-by into the watery depths. Her victims, so it is claimed, included animals as they drank from the riverbanks. Should you choose to walk along the paths of the Tees, and begin to feel uneasy, beware of what could be lurking beneath the water's surface …

Ghostly Predators of the Tees' Murky Depths

The growth of industry along the Tees at Stockton brought with it an assortment of homes, taverns and workplaces. Sadly but inevitably, the years have seen a number of people meet their untimely demise in the depths of the Tees. Fearful of the ever-present danger that the waters pose, generations of mothers have warned their infants of the terrors posed by Peg Powler, said to be the ghostly freshwater mermaid of the Tees. Secretive and mysterious, she was never to be seen; her presence was supposedly indicated by the presence of clouds of foam, and youngsters knew that those dangerous waters were to be avoided at all costs.

The Ghost of 'aad Wilson'

The Monthly Chronicle of North Country Lore and Legends for April 1891 includes the following tale:

> Some half century since, a farmer named Wilson, who had been attending Stockton market and left that town at a late hour, rather the worse for drink, to ride home to Middlesbrough, lost his way in the dark, and rode into the Tees, where he was drowned. His body was recovered soon after, but his hat, as was natural, had disappeared. His ghost was said to appear, causing terror to belated travellers. A Methodist local preacher, named John Orton, who had been at Middlesbrough conducting divine service, was returning alone one night to Stockton, when, about the locality where the farmer was lost, he met a man without any hat, to whom he bade 'Good night' but received no answer. It being near midnight and the place quite solitary Orton wondered what the man could be doing at that untimely hour. He therefore turned round and followed him, to see, if possible, where he went, for he suspected, from his appearance, that he was upon no good errand. But after tracing a few steps, he lost sight of him all of a sudden, the man disappearing, or rather vanishing, into a bush on the left-hand side of the road; and when Orton went cautiously forward to peer into the bush, there was no living creature there or near about. When he reached home, and told his wife what he had seen, she instantly exclaimed, 'Why, man, its been aad Wilson!'

Orton's son-in-law, who told us this anecdote, also gave the following account of a ghost, which he himself encountered – this time a seemingly more animalistic-looking spectre:

> One night, a few days after my father died, I was sitting in the back yard getting my pipe, when, all of a sudden, a great black dog, as large as an elephant, came and stood right before me, as motionless as a rock. I was suffering from the effects of drink at the time, and terribly out of sorts, with a head ready to split, and some feeling not unlike the horrors; but still I was in full possession of all my senses. So I determined to find out whether what I seemed to see really existed outside of me, or was within my own brain and therefore I sat watching it for about fie minutes. It stood motionless all the time my eye was steadily fixed on it. But at last, in order to satisfy myself, I moved my eye sideways, first to the left and then to the right, and finding that the dog moved either way, each time I tried the experiment, I was convinced that it only existed only in my own disordered brain.

Perhaps then this final tale should be entitled, 'Confessions of an intemperate Victorian ghost hunter'!

Stella Mary moored at Stockton's Corporation Quay.

Stockton riverside following redevelopment, viewed from the Thornaby bank.

Cervia close to the Thornaby bank.

*Paddle tug, Hero moored close
to the Thornaby bank.*

2

Haunted Town Centre Public Houses and Other Business Premises

Nightclubs, Name Changes and Paranormal Visitations

In recent years, nightclubs, bars and bistros have replaced many town centre hostelries. Name changes, closures and redevelopment schemes have brought about the demise of many long-established and traditional public houses – but in this fast-moving, ever-changing world who can say that the supernatural presence is no longer around?

Manhattan's Bar, at the northern end of Stockton's High Street, has had a number of name changes in recent years, including 'Number Nines' and 'Fitzgerald's' before taking on the current title in 2005.

The premises has a large open area with a prominent bar located in the centre. Downstairs, where toilets are situated, there was formerly a cellar bar that was popular with groups of bikers, and a steep stairwell leads to a decorated room (recently used as a sports gymnasium). On the next floor level is a vacant apartment that was formerly occupied by staff. Previous uses of the building include a gentlemen's club, workhouse and tuberculosis hospital.

Investigations by a ghost-hunting group during 2006 were hindered somewhat upon the discovery of debris from a fire on the upper floor; however, the feeling was that the soot-covered walls and boarded

The Baltic Tavern on Stockton riverside. It was demolished in 1929.

Ship Launch on Stockton riverside. This was also demolished in 1929.

The Vane Arms and Black Lion on the
spooky east side of Stockton High Street.

The King's Head Hotel in
Garbutt Street.

A view of the Doric Column and Finkle Street on market day.

up windows added to the spooky atmosphere within the building. Most of the ghostly incidents were said to have taken place in the bar area, where customers and staff witnessed numerous incidents of items moving unaided, undoubtedly a poltergeist at work! Glasses on shelves behind the bar were seen to fall to the hard floor below – oddly, though, they landed in an upright position, without breaking. Other items that were similarly moved include a cigarette lighter that had been placed on a surface in the bar area by its owner, only to disappear before being found in another part of the bar.

When the cellar bar was a popular venue for bikers, one particular rider who frequented the premises was jokingly referred to as 'a part of the furniture'. Sadly, he was fatally injured in an accident and unexplained incidents at this lower level of the building are said to be linked with him.

Staff and customers using the female toilets have reported banging on the walls of the cubicles when there was nobody else around, and the landlord recalled 'cold spots' within the former bar area. CCTV footage provided images of apparent ghostly figures behind the bar, and other reports claim that a blonde woman has been seen in the area of the central stairwell leading to the upstairs accommodation.

Rather more sinister reports are linked with the upstairs apartment, where someone woke during the night to find themselves being choked by an unseen force. Needless to say, they made a very hasty exit!

Redevelopment schemes along the east side of Stockton High Street have swept away several fine old coaching inns, as well as traditional businesses and shop frontages, but there are echoes of days gone by in the Green Dragon Yard area, located near Finkle Street.

Green Dragon Yard's Ghostly Presence

The well-known axiom, 'All human life is here', would certainly have been well merited in this bustling town centre location, which not only hosted early meetings of Baptists and Methodists but also accommodated a cockpit. Highly-prized red and black gamecocks were bred locally for combat in the central ring, while at the other end of the yard the walls of a former tithe barn echoed to the sounds of theatrical productions. Opened as a theatre in 1766, it later became a music hall before serving as a Salvation Army base and, more recently, a sweet factory.

Little wonder then that there have been ghostly sightings of the Green Dragon Inn's first landlord in the cellar below his premises. With so many comings and goings amid the hurly burly in the adjacent yard, he may well be catching up with unfinished business.

Unexplained Eerie Incidents at Other Town Centre Locations

Just a short distance away from the town's busy High Street setting, a series of strange incidents at the Bird's Nest Hotel on Yarm Lane occurred in the early 1970s. Glasses were thrown to the floor by an unseen force, furniture moved around by an ashen-faced figure and, additionally, mysterious voices were heard in the clubroom on the first floor and a showy figure was spotted on the premises.

In an attempt to explain these mysterious incidents, investigators pointed to an episode that took place some years before, when the pub was named the Old Brunswick. A fight had broken out and, during the ensuing melee, a man was thrown through a street side window and was fatally injured by a passing bus.

Further out of town, ghostly goings-on were reported at the Concord Hotel on Adam Street in the final weeks of 1996. Barry Cook, husband of the landlady, Pauline, was convinced that the unexplained incidents were down to a debt-ridden bookie's runner, who is said to have hanged himself in what used to be the coalhouse. He reported a sighting of the ghost during October 1996, and added that the haunting had been going on since they took over the premises some six years earlier.

A view of the High Street, c.1900.

A whole catalogue of unnerving incidents were attributed to the shadowy spectre, including the fondling of female staff while they were going about their business (only for the women to find no one there when they turned round), objects thrown around the kitchen, a gas ring was switched on when no one was near, a chilly draught around the pub, and most eerie of all, startling drinkers by strolling through the bar and vanishing through solid walls where doorways have been blocked up.

According to Barry, many people had witnessed the ghostly presence and he added, 'It doesn't bother me, it is one of those things. You get used to their presence. It is the living that harm you, not the dead!' A kitchen worker agreed, 'It is true. It is very friendly to me. At first I was frightened but now it doesn't bother me.'

In early 2001, the premises of an opticians in the town centre played host to a haunting when staff members began to regularly report on the exploits of a resident ghost. 'George' as he was nicknamed by employees, was said to repeatedly haunt the attic of the historic High Street store.

His exploits included turning machinery on and off intermittently, and his presence was made clear with the emergence of a powerful smell of glue; this could be linked with the days when the building was a gentleman's outfitters, and glue was used in manufacturing hats. Despite the fact that this activity would unnerve most people, the branch's manageress expressed the view that the general feeling was that George was a harmless spirit, merely checking on the building and getting up to mischievous tricks along the way!

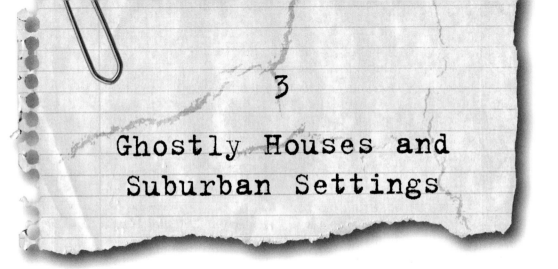

3

Ghostly Houses and Suburban Settings

SUPERNATURAL presences have the potential to make an appearance at any location and at any time – be it day or night. In some cases, there are rational explanations or obvious links with earlier events. However, other types of visitation can often defy attempts to provide us with credible answers; thus, in this respect, ghostly tales can prove resoundingly ambiguous, creating an enigma that has captivated and confused many for centuries. Older buildings, such as castles or stately homes, often feature in reported spectral sightings, but private houses are just as likely to make news as buildings accessible to the general public.

A Mysterious Spectre in Richardson Road

A family living in Richardson Road, Stockton had regular visits between 1978 and 1980 from a ghostly, cloaked figure that never showed its face. When the mysterious spectre appeared, the family's normally fearless dog crept quietly out of the room, but the appearances came to an abrupt end as preparations were made for an exorcist to call on the family in the early months of 1980.

Unexplained Sounds in Lomond Avenue, Billingham

In October 1978, press reports spoke of a 'ghost squad' called in by Stockton Borough Council to check out a house in Lomond Avenue, Billingham. Structural problems accounted for some of the strange noises that had caused the residents to move out, but other incidents defied rational explanation and officials considered enlisting assistance from a psychical research organisation in an attempt to resolve the situation.

Ghostly Shades of Dark and Light on Hardwick Estate

The early days of August 1982 brought reports of a 'lady in white' and 'a dark figure', terrifying a family on Whickham Road on the Hardwick estate. A former vicar at the local Anglican church recalled two occasions when he was called to houses in the vicinity by frightened witnesses.

Spectral figures in Dunoon Close, Ragworth

Strange happenings at a house in Dunoon Close in Ragworth perturbed the inhabitants to the extent that they eventually asked the council to move properties. Young children in the household had been upset by numerous sightings of ethereal figures appearing in their bedroom.

Ghost or no ghost? Oxbridge Cemetery

At times, some reports are not given serious consideration or are taken lightly. An article in the *Northern Echo* on 7 March 1972 stated: 'Some years ago reports of hauntings in Oxbridge Cemetery on Oxbridge Lane amused the sceptics and chilled the believers … the phantom figures of a man and his dog are said to have been seen as dusk falls.'

A Chilling Tale — Fact or Fiction?

Midway through the long summer holidays from school, Sandra Woods and her sister, Jean, were shopping one Tuesday afternoon in the large superstore on the outskirts of Stockton (at the junction of Bishopton Avenue and Bishopton Road West) when their attention was caught by a lady walking along. She looked to be aged about thirty and smiled at them before asking if they could babysit for her on Friday evenings, and, although they failed to recognise the woman, she claimed to know them and was sure of their reliability. Giving her name as Mrs Miller and a home address of Raeston Crescent, on the nearby Lauder Estate, she explained that her child was a ten-month-old boy who was extremely well behaved.

The girls' mother readily gave permission for their visit to Mrs Miller's home and when they arrived on the Friday evening they were made comfortable in the lounge and kitchen area. Before Mrs Miller left she was adamant that Sandra and Jean must not go upstairs to the baby if he cried.

For about an hour the girls watched television and were enjoying tea and biscuits when they heard the sound of a baby crying. Gentle cries grew louder and louder and the girls' dilemma increased as the crying turned almost to shrieks.

They were under strict instruction not to visit the child in his upstairs room but the crying went on until they felt that they had to intervene. Quietly, the two sisters crept upstairs and along a small landing area before gently opening the bedroom door.

The baby was still crying at the top of his voice, with bare legs kicking the air in distress, but as the girls approached the cot he quietened and held out his little arms. Sandra leaned over and picked him up but this big, bouncing baby felt cold and light in weight.

Jean took hold of the baby boy and held him close, but was surprised how light he was. Returning him to the cot, they were pleased to see him smiling contentedly and as they returned downstairs, there was no further sound from the child's bedroom.

The sisters readily agreed not to inform Mrs Miller of their upstairs visit and when she returned, as arranged, at nine o'clock, they were told that she had enjoyed a most pleasant evening whilst handing over a pound note for their services.

Returning home, the sisters updated their mother on their experiences and how they disobeyed Mrs Miller's instruction not to calm the baby. As they talked, it became clear that Jean's search in her pockets for the pound note was to no avail and they decided to wait until the following morning to see if they had dropped it on the doormat at Mrs Miller's home.

The next day, they made their way back to Raeston Crescent and rang the bell of Mrs Miller's house, but an elderly, white-haired lady answered. They were informed that there was no-one by the name of Miller at that address, and they were told firmly that they had not been baby-sitting there the previous night. Even more perplexed, the lady – Mrs Wright – explained that there was no pound note on the doormat when they returned from the Lake District late on the previous evening and the sisters were left to walk home in a bewildered state.

Back at home, their father decided to make further enquiries and when he called at the house Mrs Wright invited him into the family home, where they discussed the previous evening's events. There was a mood of sadness and embarrassment as Mr Wright began his explanation.

The previous occupants of the house were called Miller, and Mr and Mrs Wright had brought the property through a solicitor after an unpleasant episode. Mr Miller left the family home some six months after the baby was born and Norah Miller began to go out drinking in local clubs and pubs. She only left her baby for an hour or two, after he had fallen asleep, but one night she didn't return until the early hours and, tragically, the baby had died from suffocation.

Jim Woods listened, almost speechless, before asking what had happened to Mrs Miller. The answer, explained Mr Wright, was that she was severely censured at the inquest and died some six months later, from an overdose of sleeping tablets.

Mr and Mrs Wright insisted that they had been really happy in the house. On returning to his own home, Jim Woods said nothing to the girls, apart from saying that the pound note (from his own pocket) had been found on the doormat. He persuaded his daughters that the lady they had encountered was in fact the Wright's married daughter, who had been staying there during her parents' absence before returning to her own home in Leeds. Eventually he told them the truth and they were left to ponder at length about their dramatic encounter ...

Furtive Footsteps on a Busy Roadway

Reports in the late 1980s of the sound of reverberating, echoing footsteps leaving a house in Darlington Road in Hartburn, mostly heard during mid-evening, were dismissed by local sceptics. The semi-detached property at the heart of these mysterious sounds is situated between two public houses and doubters strongly suggested that these 'secret' footfalls would probably return soon after closing time if ghost watchers maintained a quiet vigil!

Unexplained Rural Encounter

A few years ago, a friend with a farming background, Keith Brown, recalled an incident in broad daylight on open farmland on the north side of Stockton. His daily routine meant that he was totally familiar with the lie of the land. As he and a companion made their way across a field towards a wicket gate in the boundary fence, they saw the figure of a man approaching the gate from the adjacent field. It seemed that they would reach the gate at about the same time as the person in the other field and, still deeply engrossed in the midst of conversation, they stood politely aside to allow him to pass through. They stood and waited, but it soon became apparent that this gesture was in vain; no figure appeared, nor was there anyone to be seen now in the neighbouring field. Could it be that this was an optical illusion, or were the minds of these two men playing mischievous tricks? Who knows? But Keith remains adamant to this day that there was a figure approaching the gate and then suddenly there wasn't!

Unnerving Home Truths

An incident in 1980 remains as clear as ever and yet there are still no explanations. My family home at that time was a detached property on the recently developed Greenvale estate (having moved in to the newly-built house in 1973). With three downstairs rooms in addition to a kitchen, cloakroom and a hallway, we were enjoying a quiet evening in front of the television in the back room when there was a loud bang from the front of the house (near the front door). Needless to say, there was an amount of trepidation as we headed through to determine the reason for this unknown sound.

A strong smell of burning rubber emerged, and so an instant check was made on an electric fire in the room. It was unplugged – as always when not in use – and closer analysis indicated that the distinctive smell was located at one specific point – in mid air – within the open space of the room. Movement to one side or the other, however short a distance, meant that the smell had gone, but if you were to return to that precise position, the odour was still there.

In the adjacent hallway, the front door was firmly locked but a picture on the wall had somehow been lifted from its nail on the wall and dropped to the carpeted floor, where it stood upright and undamaged (with the nail still embedded in the wall above). Sometime later that evening, it was discovered the clock-radio in the master bedroom – located directly above the picture – had suffered an interruption of the power supply.

With no rhyme or reason for these phenomena, a possible explanation could be linked to the death, very near to that particular time, of a close relative – but who knows?

A Vision of St Bernadette

Some years ago, a group of six women from Stockton would hold regular prayer sessions at a house in Reynoldston Avenue on the Roseworth estate; The women met every Saturday to say a prayer to Our Lady of Lourdes, and to pray for peace at a shrine. This showed the scene when St Bernadette – at the age of twelve – is reported to have seen a vision of the Virgin Mary in 1858. Since then, thousands of people have made pilgrimages to the Holy Shrine at the French town in the hope of receiving a miracle cure from their suffering.

In early March 1981, the occasion of their gathering played host to more of a spectral dimension. As they knelt before the shrine of Our Lady of Lourdes, the small group of worshippers were saying a Rosary together. They had reached the half way point when they became aware of what appeared to be a fine mist filling the room. The statue of the Virgin Mary began to fade from view, and the figure of St Bernadette moved forward as the women recalled feeling a very strong ethereal presence. One of the group later said, 'It was a little girl, a beautiful, perfect figure'.

The parish priest in Stockton was said to give a more guarded response to the report from the women worshippers and stated that he needed different sorts of proof in order to verify that the sighting was genuine.

Supernatural Episodes in the Old Merchant House

Many only older buildings appear to attract supernatural activity, so perhaps it should come as no real surprise to hear of ghostly goings-on from the Old Merchant House in Stockton's Church Road.

Staff members working in a café on the premises a few years ago reported cutlery rattled by an unseen hand, doors opening and closing of their own accord, and other light-hearted trickery. The resident chef felt more prone to these bemusing antics than other staff, but no one was said to feel threatened by these episodes.

Indeed, the sociable spook seems to have had endearing qualities and workers gave 'her' the nickname 'Elsie'. Another member of staff reported strange goings-on while vacuuming the staircase in the premises. She was unable to push the vacuum cleaner forward and suspected that the cord had become entangled on something, but when she looked back, there was nothing wrong. It seemed that 'Elsie' was playing tricks by tugging on the cord. Some staff members clearly became uneasy about her next unplanned antic. Members of staff left a chair by the window after it had been mysteriously moved there on a number of occasions, and, as no one had suffered any

harm, they decided to tolerate and accommodate for 'Elsie'.

Uncanny Incident at the King's Arms, Great Stainton

Just beyond Stockton's western boundary is the King's Arms at Great Stainton. A few years ago (and before the smoking ban came into force) an uncanny incident occured during an evening visit by a group of friends.

On arrival, the group of four adults sat at a small circular table with an ash tray in the centre. They had only been there for a short time when one of the two ladies in the group noticed that the ashtray was moving from one side of the table to the other without anyone touching either the ashtray or the table.

The movement happened again and then the lady reported seeing a very brilliant white light and sensed someone standing behind and preparing to strike her. She sprang to her feet, the light disappeared and there was no one behind her. The men folk then admitted that they had seen the ashtray move before the ladies had noticed this unexplained activity.

Soon afterwards, the group left the building, but before departure, the men asked the staff whether they had seen or heard anything strange on the premises. The answer was that if it was anything to do with an ashtray then they had heard of it from other customers. They were also informed that the pub was built on top of a burial ground.

Spirits from the Coaching Age

There may be few reminders of the coaching era in Stockton and Yarm but a few miles to the south, where the A19 and A172 routes converge, the Cleveland Tontine Inn holds a whole host of memories from those colourful times.

Following the opening of the Thirsk-Yarm turnpike and an increase in traffic, there were calls for an inn to cater for coaches. Subscriptions opened on 1 February 1804 and contributions from local gentry, farmers and business people soon raised the sum of £2,500. Building work began on 13 July 1804 and by 5 September a daily postal service was in operation.

The name 'Tontine' is connected with Lorenzo Tonti from Naples, who devised the arrangement in 1653 where shares were passed, on the death of an individual shareholder, to other remaining shareholders. The last surviving contributor, or shareholder, eventually inherited the whole amount.

Expansion of the railway network brought a downturn in trade and the Cleveland Tontine was acquired by N.K. Punshon as a family home, before Cameron's Brewery Ltd bought the property. They operated it as a high-quality roadhouse with restaurant, ballroom and cellar bar. Members of the McCoy family bought the Tontine in 1976 and continue to run a highly successful restaurant business in the splendid setting.

Unexplained phenomena are mainly centred on the attic area. In earlier times, two young children used to play here and people in the room below have heard the sound of feet pattering across the ceiling.

On other occasions objects have moved under their own volition while some people have detected the presence of a man in the same area who seems to be very protective towards the children – to such an extent that he is said to exert downward pressure to prevent anyone climbing the steep stairs into the attic. Ghostly legs have been spotted in Room 3 of the building, heading towards the bathroom, and a spectral figure has been seen in the adjacent gardens.

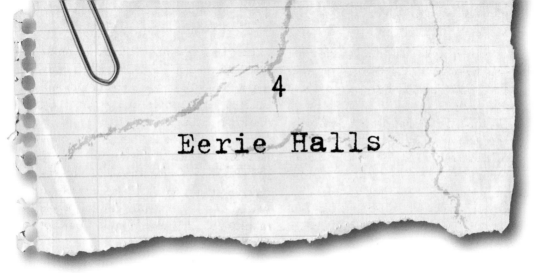

4

Eerie Halls

STOCKTON'S growth as a centre of industrial production during the second half of the nineteenth century led to the construction of a number of large private residences around the perimeter of the township. Originally set amidst farmland and open countryside, they are now surrounded by recent housing developments; yet that touch of grandeur is still in evidence and in several cases, so are the resident ghosts.

The Tragic Ghost of a Young Servant Girl

Norton House, home of the Hogg family, stood on the east side of Norton Green until 1934 and a second floor window on the east side was always covered by shutters.

During the 1860s, a young female servant was made pregnant by one of the visiting guests and, overcome by shame, she decided to end the pregnancy. Aware that facepowder used by the ladies of the house contained tincture of arsenic, she poured a quantity into a glass of water and it turned into acid.

Within minutes of drinking some of the liquid, the poor girl was in terrible pain and in a vain attempt to attract help she pulled both curtains and shutters of the bedroom.

From that time, until demolition of the building in 1934, red shutters covered the window and even though the building disappeared, the ghostly spirit of the unfortunate servant is said to have been seen over the years in the locality.

Mystery Death and a Restless Spirit

The Chapman family were major land and property owners in the Northern area during the late eighteenth and early nineteenth centuries. Marmaduke Chapman was based at Townend Farm and as well as his farm work he also served as a churchwarden at St Mary's Church, Norton, where Revd Christopher Anstey was vicar.

On an autumn day in 1806, servants working both indoors and outdoors heard a violent argument between Marmaduke and his wife, Rachel. There was no lunch-time refreshment for the household and servants were dispersed on different tasks around the village.

Soon afterwards, a group of farm workers in meadows at Crooksbarn saw a plume of smoke drifting from the barn at Chapman's farm and raced across to extinguish the fire.

Burning straw was put out but close by, among straw that was not burnt, their relief turned to horror when they uncovered the body of Mrs Chapman.

The local officer of the law and other investigators soon arrived on the scene and wondered why Mr Chapman had not been present at the fire. Marmaduke Chapman was accompanying the group to the scene of the blaze in the barn when he made an excuse to fetch a coat and hat. As the others waited in the hallway there was the sound of a gunshot from the adjacent parlour and when they rushed into the room, Marmaduke lay dead on the floor with a pistol by his head.

After further investigations, doctors found that Rachel Chapman had suffered a broken neck as the result of a fall, and a number of broken stair rods marked the scene of her accident. The exact circumstances of the incident remained unknown and Marmaduke's possible involvement was never clear. He was buried in an unmarked grave.

Rachel's ghostly spirit is said to be present in the locality. A sighting in 1983 resulted in a car swerving and then mounting Hermitage Green as the driver avoided 'a small dark figure that appeared suddenly in the car's headlights.' A number of other sightings have been reported down the years, with a long-skirted female figure wearing a poke-bonnet spotted in the area between St Mary's Church wall and Hermitage Place.

By the early 1700s, land holding on Stockton's northern edge was made up of several large farms, including two named Grassy Nook and Coxs. During the 1740s, corn was in short supply and poor harvests and flooding made the situation even worse.

Food was extremely scarce when a gypsy and her baby came to the door of Grassy Nook to request rations and the lady of the house, showing a cruel lack of humanity, ordered the gypsy to 'be gone'. Soon afterwards, the farmer and his workers discovered the bodies of the gypsy and her child.

When the gypsy family arrived to collect the bodies, a curse was put on the lady of 'Grassy Nook' that she would not rest for eternity. The restless spirit of the 'Grey Lady' remained on the site along with the gypsy woman when the farm buildings were pulled down and replaced by the imposing late Victorian house that stands there today. For a time, the fine new residence was without a name and it was given the name Kiora Hall by Lieutenant John Trenchman when he moved into the property.

The story behind his choice of name is quite intriguing. Lieutenant Trenchman was serving with the 52nd

Kiora Hall on Ragpath Lane in Stockton: the reported haunting site of Stockton's Grey Lady and the gypsy woman.

Elmwood Youth and Community Centre on Greens Lane – reportedly home to a spectral servant girl.

Foot Regiment during the Maori wars over land rights, when his troops were surprisingly cornered during a Battle at Gate Pa. Facing an impossible position, the totally unexpected happened when fighting suddenly stopped and the Maori foes laid down their weapons and offered the lieutenant's men food and drink. On his return to Stockton, Lieutenant Trenchman used his Maori word for 'welcome' – 'Kiora' – as the name for his home on the west side of Ragpath Lane at Roseworth.

During the Second World War, Kiora Hall became the headquarters for service-men and a site for anti-aircraft guns. In recent years, it has been used as a commu-nity base for Stockton Borough Council, with a host of activities for all age and abil-ity groups – with the ghosts of the 'Grey Lady', the gypsy woman and Lieutenant Trenchman still casting a ghostly eye over the building.

Railway development on Stockton's western side, and its subsequent industrial development, brought about the arrival of several new properties in Hartburn, includ-ing Elmwood at the junction of Darlington Road and Green Lane. Few records are available, but what is derived from details in Street and Trade Directories appears to suggest that Lewis Dodshon was the builder and first owner of the premises in 1880.

Twelve years later, Elmwood was leased, and in 1897, the building was sold to Henry Grant Spence. It remained the property of the Spence family until the mid-1920s, with Colonel Gilbert A. Spence as owner from 1914 to 1924.

The Kitching family took over the build-ing from 1926 to 1939 and ICI. Ltd occupied it during the war years. They added out-buildings, including lead-lined laboratories, but in 1952 Elmwood was leased to Durham County Council for use as a youth centre and in 1968 it was bought by Teeside County Borough Council, before take-over by Cleveland County Council in 1974.

As with Kiora Hall, Elmwood is now run by Stockton Borough Council as a community centre, and although most of the original furniture was removed and transferred to Windlestone Hall near Bishop Auckland and Preston Hall Museum, its spacious rooms, bays and decorative staircase have plenty of character. There is a spectral presence, too, in the form of a ghostly housemaid who hanged herself in an upper room. She has reportedly been seen in her servant clothes making fleeting appearances at windows in the highest section of the building.

Situated at the eastern end of Harlsey Road, Hartburn Lodge was built for the Raimes family in 1903. This is evident from the carving of the initials and figures, 'FR 1903 MR carved in stone above the main entrance and in the wood panelling of the entrance hall.

It was known locally as 'Bootpolish Hall' and gossip among local villagers suggested that the owner made his fortune either be selling boot polish from his car or by retailing black metal polish from premises in Stockton. The spectre that lurks in Hartburn Lodge is said to haunt the upper rooms, and is allegedly a pilot from the Second World War. A notable visitor on 4 September 1911 was the Salvation Army leader and the *North Eastern Evening Gazette* reported the folowing:

General Booth in the North. The need for a new law to deal with vagrants. A representative of the *North Eastern Daily Gazette* had a few minutes interesting chat with General Booth at Hartburn Lodge where he has this weekend been the guest of Mr & Mrs Fred Raimes during his visit to Stockton …

During the years in between the First World War and the Second World War, there were a number of owners and between 1939 and 1945 it was a base for Barrage Balloon personnel. In fact, it is probable that military personnel were involved with more important business than was suggested at the time. They would co-ordinate action at Goosepool and Thornaby aerodromes if these locations were bombed and a twenty-four-hour armed guard was posted at the building during the war years. On one occasion, it seems that a careless sentry caused his gun to misfire, with the bullet ending up lodged in the interior wall of the entrance lodge.

After the Second World War, Hartburn Lodge was bought by Mr and Mrs Murray who lived there until 1954, when they sold the property to Durham County Council. It was used as a nursery during the 1960s

The main entrance to Elmwood.

Entrance gate and lodge to Hartburn Lodge on Harlsey Road.

Gatekeeper's lodge and entrance on Harlsey Road

Front door and porch of Hartburn Lodge.

and '70s, and then, after a gap of eighteen months, it became a hostel for mentally handicapped children in 1979.

Much of the interior remains unaltered, and it retains most of its original features, although some partition walls have been added to form extra bedrooms and a staff office. Its beautiful fireplaces, wood panelling and wall friezes are still in place within the impressive main building, while a stable block and mature trees add to the eerie grandeur of the setting.

The south front of Hartburn Lodge.

The drawing room, Hartburn Lodge.

The Raimes family, pictured in the grounds of Hartburn Lodge..

Oak room, Hartburn Lodge.

The entrance hall at Hartburn Lodge.

Stables at Hartburn Lodge.

South west view of Hartburn Lodge, showing its conservatory.

5

Spooky Goings-on in Norton, Billingham and Wynyard

THOUGH it is now a northern suburb of Stockton, Norton's origins are much earlier than its riverside neighbour, with evidence of occupation stretching back some 15,000 years.

During the early 1980s, a pagan cemetery was discovered alongside Mill Lane and close to the site of Norton Mill. In total, 125 burials were identified dating from the period between AD 550 and 610, and, during the mid-1990s, a further eighty-three graves were discovered only about 200yds from the earlier burial ground. This later cemetery is believed to contain at least 600 burials and dates from the arrival of Christianity during the early 600s AD. Experts believe that it probably served the neighbouring settlements of Stockton, Hartburn and Preston as well as Norton until the parish church of St.Mary the Virgin was built.

This splendid church has a rare Saxon crossing tower and a range of other architectural styles in different parts of the cruciform building. The adjacent village has probably been located around the green since the eleventh century and in more recent times it has been encroached on by the vicarage (rebuilt in 1767) and the central group of buildings including the National School of 1833. Many of the properties around the village green date from the eighteenth century with several exceptions, including Red House, Norton Hermitage and the Quaker Meeting House (founded in 1671 and rebuilt in 1902-3).

Trees line both sides of Norton's High Street, which has a variety of impressive eighteenth-century houses and cottages,

Tower and northern section of St Mary's Church.

View of St Mary's Church from the southwest showing later additions.

Interior of St Mary's Church showing the nave crossing with pulpit, rood screen and candle chandeliers in about 1910.

Interior, Norton Church, Stockton-on-Tees

Church of St Mary the Virgin viewed from the southeast in about 1900.

School Board Tablet.

The National School.

while Fox's Almshouses, at the southern end, gives a clue to earlier local industries. Completed in 1897, they were endowed in the will of John Henry Fox, owner of one of the two breweries that operated in Norton during the late nineteenth century. The ironworks of Warner Brothers is remembered for casting the bell in 1856 that was used in the lock tower of Westminster. Warners closed in 1916 but another set of well-known industrial buildings, at Norton Mill, survived until the Second World War.

At one time there were seven water mills along Billingham Beck but Norton Mill, with a reference in the Bishop of Durham's Boldon Book of 1183, is the best-known. The mill was built in the eighteenth century and the nearby mill pond was popular with skaters during freezing weather. Perhaps they were unaware of the series of chilling events linked with the mill's dramatic ghostly goings-on.

Fox's Almshouses, Norton High Street.

Tablet on the gable of Fox's Almshouses

Central entrances to Fox's Almshouses

This tale is described in a lengthy and rambling, but no less terrifying, account of events by 'An Old Stocktonian'. In rather shorter form, the action centres around a wedding party held at Norton Mill for the daughter of the miller, a Mr Thrattles.

Celebrations went well. Eating, drinking and general merriment continued through the day and into the evening towards midnight. A final game of cards was called for and agreed before the guests dispersed to their own homes, but proceedings were dramatically interrupted by a gentleman named Benson. He insisted on recalling an incident that followed a previous gathering at Christmas time.

Leaving the mill buildings, he was crossing the adjacent garden area when conversation turned to the subject of the death of 'poor Miller Gossack'. As he paused at the spot at which the fatality occured, Benson and his companions saw a dark figure heading their way and though he blurted out a greeting, 'the mysterious figure shot past us as quickly as the shadow of a wind-driven cloud. It turned its hideous glare at us,

Norton Green and duck pond.

and said, in a sharp, husky, sepulchral tone, "Good night, gentlemen!"'

Before the terrifying apparition disappeared from view, the group of trembling onlookers saw flames pouring from its eyes, nose and ears. The eyewitness admitted that he and his companions 'were transfixed to the earth with fear and bewilderment' before managing to continue their homeward journey.

This dramatic episode, as told by Benson, left the audience dumbstruck until Miller Thrattles revived the convivial atmosphere with defiant words and a call for more card games and a round of drinks. According to Benson, the evening's proceedings at Norton Mill were almost at an end when,

a rustling, hissing sound was heard at the end of the long table nearest the window, and there arose from the floor as it were, the same horrid dark figure that the three men saw in the lane ... Every person

Mill Lane, leading to the site of Norton Mill, close to the site of over 100 ancient burials.

present saw the weird figure, but no one moved or spoke … as it glared down upon them with its flaming fiendish glances.

Following Benson's account, the alarming figure is said to have moved away, with a ghoulish parting shot of, 'Good night gentlemen!' in the same hollow, terrifying voice that it uttered previously in the lane nearby. Gripped by incredulity and fear, the company were dumbstruck before Thrattles rallied the spirits of those present. In subdued tones, Benson and Thrattles discussed the origins of the fearsome apparition and it seems that it all stemmed from an incident at Christmas time 1879, when George Gossack was miller at Bishop's Mill. Everyone was in festive spirits and one of Gossack's sons, George, a medical student, decided to play a practical joke on an unsuspecting maidservant. He had brought home a human skeleton that was hung by wires in the dining room linen cupboard and when the maid entered the room she was asked to fetch some dinner napkins.

As the maid opened the cupboard doors, the skeleton, instead of hanging in front of her, caught on the door and then seized her by the neck. The unfortunate servant collapsed into a coma, later being committed to care in Sedgefield Asylum.

Within days, villagers had turned against George Gossack and forced him out of the Unicorn Inn, in a way not unlike a lynch mob. As he made his way down Mill Lane, he was brutally attacked by an axe-wielding stranger and a single blow left him fatally injured. The murderer was soon apprehended; he turned out to be the maid's grief-stricken father. In July 1880, the maid's father was hanged at Durham Gaol to pay for his crime; however, it is the ghost of his victim, George Gossack, that is said to put in the odd spectral appearance at the eastern end of Mill Lane.

Bishop's Mill in Norton operated until 1910 but the mill buildings were struck by bombs from a Heinkel III on 1 June 1940 and they had to be pulled down in 1943. The site was excavated in 1979, before construction of the A19 route along Billingham Bottoms.

Military Men and Ghostly Manoeuvres

Close to the centre of Norton, the Red Lion at Harland Place, is full of atmosphere and interest. It was operated as a hostelry in the second half of the nineteenth century, and in the 1920s it was extended into the next-door property, which had previously been the Grey family's home.

Ground at the rear of the building is overlooked by Norton Medical Centre and over the years, people living or working in the area have reported hearing a sharp explosion followed by a dull thud. These sinister sounds have been linked with events at the Grey family home in 1812, when a celebratory ball was in full swing.

Guests of honour included Lieutenant Henry Stapylton, a veteran of Wellington's campaigns in Spain, and officers from the Loyal Stockton Volunteers, but during the evening proceedings became distinctly unpleasant. A quarrel broke out between Lieutenant Stapylton and young Thomas Grey, a Coronet of Horse in the Volunteers, who was accused of making insulting remarks about the veteran officer's uniform and military service.

Stapylton's response was to accuse Grey of cowardice and the upshot was that a duel was arranged for the following morning. The location chosen was the orchard at the rear of the house and when shots rang out from the duelling pistols, Grey fell to the

The Red Lion Inn, Harland Place, home to a plethora of sinister sounds.

The rear of the Red Lion Inn.

ground mortally wounded. Stapylton fled the scene and rejoined the army, only to be killed in action on St Valentine's Day in 1814.

In recent years there have been reported sightings of a cloaked figure at the foot of the stairs at the rear of the Red Lion and these could be linked with an incident on 20 July 1964. The landlord's daughter, Hannah Rowntree, was attempting to evict a drunken customer from the building when he pushed her. She fell heavily and later died from her injuries. At various times since then staff at the pub have experienced feelings of being watched as well as seeing a dark figure in the cellar and finding objects in a locked cellar, scattered across the floor.

Property at the corner of Holly Street and Norton Road, which plays host to raincoat-clad spectres!

Domestic Visitations

Strange goings-on have been reported on numerous occasions at a house on the corner of Norton Road and Holly Street. During a brief residence in the property a few years ago, the lady of the house reported seeing a man in a long raincoat at the top of the staircase. By the time she had roused her husband, the spectre had vanished into thin air. The next occupants of the house had similar sightings but the ghostly incidents ended after the property was exorcised.

Ghostly Hounds

Sightings of 'ghostly hounds' have been reported from many parts of the country. At times, particularly during stormy conditions, one's mind can play tricks, as I know from personal experience when walking the family dog across open fields in Hartburn on the west side of Stockton. Distant lines of hawthorn hedge, along the upper edge of a ridge, can suddenly become a line of charging horsemen or animals against a darkening skyline.

Eyewitness accounts from the Blakeston Lane area of Norton are even more chilling. A local driver was returning to the kennels at Blakeston and had just passed the site of Blakeston Hall when his wife screamed a warning and braced herself for a collision with a large, dark animal in the road ahead. As their car screeched to a halt and after they had recovered their composure, the man and his wife retraced the short distance to the sighting, but found no evidence of the creature.

This report is typical of several from the same location and attempts to explain the phantom 'hound' point to a dramatic episode involving the South Durham Hunt. Meeting

Blakeston Lane, where it has been reported that spectral animals appear in the middle of the road without warning.

drop into the nearby quarry. Then, of course, there have been reported sightings, in more recent times, of the so-called 'Durham puma' ... but that just deepens the mystery surround this ghostly creature.

Curious Customs and Churchyard Ghosts

Churchyards are fascinating locations with many features that shed light on earlier events and individuals from earlier days. Apart from gravestones there are often monuments and memorials, perhaps a holy well or even a plague pit – all providing a wealth of detail about life and death in the particular parish.

Yew trees often provide a sombre and sobering feature in country churchyards and, until about a century ago, local menfolk assembled on St Mark's Eve (24 April) for a strange enactment.

It was widely believed in northern England that on that date, between 11 p.m. and 1 a.m., the spirits of people who would die during the following twelve months haunted the churchyard. A variation on this practice involved spodomancy – or 'riddling the ashes' – when ashes were left on the household hearth overnight on St Mark's Eve. According to local folklore, close examination of the ashes the next day would reveal the footprint of anyone who was going to die during the next year.

During the nineteenth century some men folk kept a graveyard vigil for very different reasons. Bodysnatchers became such a menace that large stone slabs were often used to prevent bodies being taken out of their graves, and male friends and relatives took turns in watching the grave for a number of nights after interment.

at Wynyard Hall in 1871, to mark the opening of the branch line across Thorpe Viaduct. The pack of hounds picked up a scent that led them through South Wood and across Wolviston Road into Crow Wood, near Blakeston Hall. The chase continued towards Low Middlefield Farm and Durham Road, with a clear sighting of the fox across open ground ahead. With success seemingly within reach, disaster struck.

Suddenly, the fox doubled back, spinning sharply away from the edge of a precipitous drop into a water-filled quarry, but the pursuing hounds were not so alert. Six couples of hounds plunged into the depths before whippers-in stopped the rest of the pack and it was a saddened Hunt that made its way slowly back to Wynyard Hall.

Over the years, speculation has focused on the nature of the apparition and the reasons for its sudden appearance. Some reports suggest that it is a fox, rather than a hound, but the majority support the claim that it is a hound giving warning of the dangerous

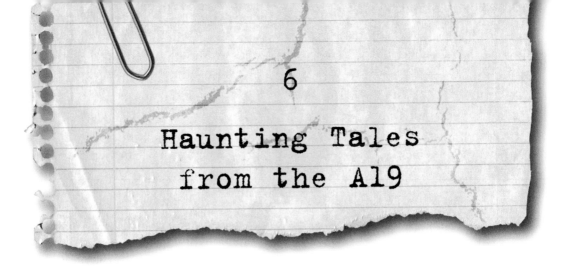

6

Haunting Tales from the A19

A Bishop's Curse on a Modern Road System

Slicing through low-lying ground between Stockton and Billingham, the north and south-bound carriageways of the A19 play a vital role in Teesside's transport network system. The four and a half mile section of roadway that make up the Billingham bypass opened in November 1982 at a cost of £17 million and greatly relieved congestion in the residential area of Billingham.

Work on the bypass had begun in July 1980 but just before completion of the lengthy project there was an unexpected complication. The bridge that carried Stockton ring road, the A1027 over the A19, started to sink into the marshland; this untimely turn of events came as no surprise to some inhabitants of Norton.

They laid the cause of the sinking flyover firmly and squarely on the 'Bishop's curse'. For centuries the Bishop of Durham held sway over territory that extended, on the southern boundary, to the River Tees, and his officials collected payment from travellers at a number of tollbooths and toll bridges. The Bishop's curse was said to have been put on the head of anyone who

left the Palatinate without paying the toll. Substance was added to this claim when it was found that supporting piles driven under the bridge had unearthed the stone-work of the medieval Bishop's Mill.

Smuggling Spectres at the Flaming Stump

Closer to the River Tees, with a backdrop of the A19 Tees Viaduct, low-lying land is covered in industrial estates and the Portrack Marsh Nature Reserve. There is no trace nowadays of a once-busy inn with a splendid name – the Flaming Stump – that boasted a superb wall frieze in its Angel Room.

Customers were probably, for the most part, anything but angelic, as this isolated riverside hostelry gained a reputation as a favourite haunt of smugglers. It seems that they transferred illicit goods up the hill to Holm House for storage in cellars, while excise men took refreshment in the Flaming Stump.

Straightening of the river channel and a new road linking Stockton and Middlesbrough brought a loss in trade and closure of the inn. A cottage was added to the original building and the enlarged property became Portrack Grange Farm. It continued in use until the late 1950s, and although there were calls for its preservation because of its historical importance, demolition followed soon afterwards, and then, it would seem, the hauntings followed.

Within living memory, local people believed that the building was haunted and passed this isolated setting with great caution. Perhaps they were only smugglers' fabricated stories – put about to distract attention from their activities – or maybe there was, and still is, an eerie, unexplained atmosphere at Portrack.

Wynyard's Majestic Hall and Ghostly Memories

The name 'Wynyard' may be derived from two Anglo Saxon words: 'winn' meaning meadow and 'yeard' denoting enclosure, and the present spelling of the hall has remained unaltered since the sixteenth century.

Early owners included the Conyers and Claxton families, before Wynyard was purchased by John Tempest in 1742 for the sum of £8,200. On his death it passed to his nephew, Henry Vane, who had to take the family name of Tempest in order to inherit. In 1813 his daughter took over and six years later she married Lord Stewart, who became third Marquess of Londonderry in 1921.

Wynyard flourished under the third Marquess and his wife. He had a notable military and diplomatic career as well as building an extensive mining network in the north east (with much of it focused on Seaham).

Between 1822 and 1827 a new hall was constructed to designs by Philip Wyatt, but two thirds of the building were destroyed in a disastrous fire that broke out on 19 February 1841.

The fourth and fifth Marquises took little interest in Wynyard (although the German Chancellor, Otto von Bismarck, was entertained there in 1883) but when Charles, sixth Marquess, took over, politicians and royal visitors returned to Wynyard.

This trend continued under the seventh Marquess but when Robin, eighth Marquess, inherited in 1949, he faced increasing problems with outlying farms and estate buildings in a poor state of repair. During the 1980s the hall was made available for hire by the public but in mid-1987 the Londonderry's severed all connections with Wynyard when the entire estate was sold to Sir John Hall of Cameron Hall Developments.

Sir John's daughter, Allison Antonopoulos, masterminded the transformation of Wynyard into a top hotel, wedding and conference centre that opened its doors to guests in 2007.

The grounds that were laid out in 1822 include the late eighteenth-century style stone Lion Bridge, the Wellington Obelisk (erected in 1827 and standing 127ft high) to celebrate a visit by the Duke, a pair of classical temples, and gate lodges with cast-iron gates and railings. Late in 2010, Sir John Hall announced plans to enhance Wynyard's surroundings with the addition of a £2 million rose garden.

Wynyard's Ghostly Grey Lady

Conversations with estate staff in the early 1980s provided details of a series of intriguing unexplained incidents, most of which centred around a 'Grey Lady'.

On one occasion, the security alarm sounded at the hall and an intrepid member of staff decided to search all rooms on the ground floor level without waiting for police assistance. He had reached the old kitchens when the door inexplicably banged shut and was locked… Yet the key was still hanging on the wall. There was no possible reason why the door should have shut (of its own accord) or why it had locked, but my confidant goes down in local folklore as the man who locked 'the Grey Lady 'in the kitchen.

On the ground floor, the same employee was making his way along the bottom passage and opened the door of the game larder to deposit various items. As he turned to make his way back to his van, the door banged shut behind him and the bolt was fastened on the inside. This meant that he had to go another way round to get back into the larder, and again there was no reason why the door should have closed.

In the same area of the hall, the member of staff turned a key in the door leading into the kitchen/larder only for it to suddenly swing open of its own accord. Inside the room the temperature was very cold – as in an ice larder – and the workman suggested – perhaps tongue in cheek – that the Grey Lady was feeling rather lonely and wanted some company on this occasion.

This series of incidents may be linked with the tragic drowning of a lady in the lake near the hall. Fifteen or so years previously, the lake had been cleaned out and the theory is that her spirit had been disturbed. Reported sightings of the ghostly female have centred on the Lion Bridge – sometimes in a carriage drawn by horses – and on one occasion the witness had to hold back his dogs, which were snarling at the passing apparition.

On another occasion, a ghostly male figure was observed walking along Sandy Lane near 'the Golden Gates' on the south side of the estate. It closely resembled a man who had been fatally injured in an accident on this location some fifteen or twenty years earlier.

Closer analysis of these reports indicated that most of the supernatural sightings took place in November and this conclusion is echoed on a much wider scale on the national stage of spectral visitations.

A Galaxy of Ghosts at Preston Hall

Preston-on-Tees is mentioned in the Bishop of Durham's Boldon Book of 1183 when land in the area was farmed by Adam, son of Walter de Stockton, Orm, son of Crockett and William, son of Utting. In later centuries, landholders included the Seton, Sayers and Witham families before Sir John Eden of Windlestone assumed ownership in 1722.

During 1820, land at Preston was sold to David Burton Fowler of Yarm and in 1825 he built a plain brick property. Less than a year later a section of the Stockton and Darlington line was completed close to the boundary of the parkland. On his death, the estate passed to his great nephew, Marshall Robinson, who assumed the family name and it continued in the Fowler family until 1882 when a Prussian, Emil Hugo Oscar Robert Ropner, purchased the estate.

The Ropner family made an important contribution to Stockton's development – particularly through their shipbuilding business, which provided employment for large numbers of local folk. Colonel Ropner, as he was then known, presented a public park to the townspeople in 1890. As Sir Robert Ropner, he made alterations to the family home at Preston Hall. The addition of a heavy stone porch and domed conservatory transferred the frontage from the side overlooking the river to the section facing on to the Stockton – Yarm road (A135).

Wynyard Hall – main entrance.

Wynyard estate – the former dairy.

Preston Hall Museum.

A section of rail track from the Stockton
and Darlington line, outside Preston Hall.

Leonard, the youngest of Sir Robert's five sons, inherited Preston Hall in 1924 and on his death, in 1937, the premises were taken over by Ashmore Benson and Pease Ltd. Plans to develop the parkland with housing and amenities were turned down in 1944 and in July 1947 Stockton Corporation took over the estate and hall for development as a public park and museum.

The museum was opened on 3 June 1953 by Alderman C.W. Allinson with impressive displays of arms, armour, powder flasks, pewter and snuff boxes, which had been left to the Borough of Stockton by Colonel G.O. Spence. Alterations during the winter months of 1968/9 included the construction of galleries illustrating social life from 1750-1900 and in the early 1970s two outstanding works of art were rediscovered in the upper floor of the hall. Experts identified them as 'Mustering of the Warrior Angels' completed in 1833 by Joseph Mallard William Turner, and 'The Diceplayers' by the French artist Georges de la Tour (1593-1652). More recent developments include the creation of a North Country street of the 1890s with specialist shops and craftsmen's workshops and the opening, in 1991, of Europe's largest butterfly farm, 'Butterfly World'.

Throughout the years, members of staff at Preston Hall have reported a number of spectral sightings at different locations around this atmospheric building.

Many of these incidents took place close to the front porch and on ground outside, where a ghostly highwayman has been spotted. There are suggestions that this presence may be linked with the Stockton – Darlington railway line which ran alongside the roadway.

A Grey Lady has been seen making her way down the main staircase in the hall. Again, there is no clear indication of her identity but some investigators suggest that she may have been a member of the owning family who became pregnant by one of the estate workers but later lost the baby.

Part of the hall which is now known as 'the dungeon' was originally an old wine cellar, and it is here that a lady has been seen with her dog walking through the wall and down the corridor. Ghost-hunting groups have made several visits to the hall, and it is in this area of the building that people have told of anxiety and disquiet, along with a strong inclination to move out of 'the dungeon'.

Adjoining the main building, part of the former stables area has been converted into a Toy Gallery and it is here and along the main corridor back to the hall that sightings of the Grey Lady feelings of being watched have been reported.

Preston Hall was closed in November 2010 for extensive alterations and refurbishment financed by Lottery funding, with reopening scheduled for March 2012.

7

Supernatural Settings in Eaglescliffe and Egglescliffe

LOCATED approximately halfway between Stockton-on-Tees and Yarm, Eaglescliffe owes its existence largely to nineteenth-century railway expansion. The original route of the Stockton and Darlington railway was on the east side, but the arrival of the Leeds Northern line in 1852 saw the transfer of the Stockton and Darlington to a new line from 25 January 1853, with Eaglescliffe as an important interchange point.

Until this time there had been no station at Eaglescliffe and local folklore indicates that when the new buildings were constructed near Preston Junction, a sign writer was detailed to paint the name. Unfortunately, so the tale runs, the piece of paper that he was given had the name wrongly spelled and so it is that the original village remains Egglescliffe while the new development close to the railway station is Eaglescliffe.

Spectral Incidents in the Sportsman's Hotel

The area close to Yarm Road and The Avenue saw construction of several large residential properties for local industrialists and businessmen while the imposing building that now houses the Sportsman's Hotel in Station Road began life, in 1892, as the waiting room for Eaglescliffe railway station.

In keeping with its name, the hotel is home to a number of sports teams and leisure activities, but it is also the setting for a sequence of supernatural incidents. Gas bottles turned off in the cellar when no one was there, empty glasses left unattended after everything has been cleared away, the thump of darts on the dartboard and the creaking of the women's lavatory door opening and closing when the premises were locked and empty – all totally unexpected and unexplained phenomena.

At other times there have been spectral sightings, as when a cleaner saw a pair of feet – and then no one there. At this point she promptly dashed from the building! On another occasion, the landlady was sitting at a table in the upstairs flat when she saw the apparition of a woman dressed in a dark-coloured Victorian dress and a pinafore staring at her. Her gaze was not frightening – more friendly. There are, sadly, no clues to her identity or reason for her appearance.

The Sportsman's Hotel, Eaglescliffe.

Spooky Images at the Radiographic Factory

On the outskirts of Eaglescliffe a shadowy, white-shirted figure has made several unscheduled appearances at the Intex Radiographic Factory, on the local trading estate. Stories of a ghostly figure have persisted since the company moved to the site in 1969 and all four lady members of staff in the darkroom have had first-hand encounters with the silhouette of the Victorian gentleman.

Tudor-Style Travellers

Close by on Urlay Nook Road, bus drivers travelling to or from Eaglescliffe have reported seeing groups of people in 'Tudor-style costume' walking across the road above the present level of the highway. There is no evidence to indicate who these strange figures might be but such spectral sightings often take place near a battlefield

Rear of the Sportsman's Hotel.

(such as Marston Moor, near York). The only local setting of this nature was the skirmish around Yarm Bridge during the English Civil War, in 1643.

The modern road surface is considerably lower than it was in earlier times and this would explain the gap between today's road level and the figures seen by passing drivers.

It may be only a stone's throw from the A135 and Yarm's bustling High Street, but Egglescliffe village green has retained an atmosphere of peace and calm. There is no sign, today, of the two wells, quoits pitch and wooden stocks, but the stone cross was

Rose Cottage on the north side of Egglescliffe Green.

A group of children in front of Ivy Cottages on Egglescliffe Green.

Egglescliffe village green.

Line of children standing at the end of a quoits pitch on Egglescliffe village green.

Group of children in centre of Egglescliffe green with pinfold in the background.

restored in 1984 at the upper end of the sloping green, while surrounding brick-built cottages add to the air of timelessness.

Ghostly Goings-on at the Pot and Glass

Church Road leads from the green to high ground overlooking the River Tees, with the impressive stonework of St John's Church on the north side and the Pot and Glass below the churchyard on the south side. This splendid village inn is more than 300 years old and was known in its early days as the Pot and Pipe.

In view of this longevity, it perhaps should come as no surprise that there is plenty of talk about ghosts at the Pot and Glass. Most of this centres around a supposed tunnel that ran between the pub and church, with witnesses reporting the sounds of doom-laden organ music even though the church was empty and there was no human presence.

St John's Church itself has a fine array of woodwork dating from Bishop Cosin's period of office, including screen, pews, chancel stalls and an eighteenth-century three-decker pulpit.

Interior of St John's Church, Egglescliffe.

Egglescliffe and a Series of Vivid Supernatural Encounters

Butts Lane links the A135 Yarm Road with Egglescliffe village and takes its name from the days when local men folk had to practise their skills with crossbows on targets in an adjacent field. During recent years, land beside the roadway has been developed with housing, including properties adjacent to Yarm Road on St Margaret's estate. A bungalow in this area has been the focus for a number of dramatic ghostly appearances.

Within just two weeks of moving into the family home, the ghostly lady made her first appearance. Whilst sitting in her lounge, the lady owner of the house saw the apparition glide past a window looking on to the hall before peering round the door. Though she did admit a fear of horror films, the home-owner was not frightened by the spectre, who was wearing 'an off-white cloak with hood or cowl that covered her face'.

There were more possible indications of the presence of the ghostly female at various times during evenings – sometimes when the television set was switched on and on other occasions when the screen was blank. Intriguingly, the householder's husband failed to see the apparition and was even more dumbfounded when his wife suggested to the ghostly vision, 'Why

St John's Church, Egglescliffe.

1969 Stony Bank, Eaglescliffe,

don't you come in? I want to talk to you,' however, on each occasion, the spectre disappeared from view along the hallway.

The supernatural visitor appeared for three evenings out of seven for several months and then, after several months of non-appearance, she made a dramatic return. An elderly relative was staying at the family home when the apparition appeared in the doorway with such realism that the visiting relative took her to be a neighbour or friend and called out, 'she's just gone out the back to the freezer'.

When the householder returned to the room, she was asked if the friend/neighbour had found her – and she then explained in detail to her relative about the ghostly visitor. Describing the spectre as young and very attractive, the witness was prepared when she made another unscheduled appearance at 4 a.m. Due to the fact that the elderly lady was suffering from hearing problems and arthritis, she was about to call for help when the apparition soothingly said, 'Don't worry. Keep calm. Everything will be alright.'

There were further sightings by family members and friends – while others remained steadfastly unconvinced.

As for explanations, there was no definite indication as to the identity of the ghostly female but the land in this sector was formerly part of the estate around St Margaret's House. This large mansion was demolished to make way for the housing development, and the bungalow stands on part of the original walled garden and close to the line of the driveway leading to the hall. A lodge is still standing beside the nearby A135.

The most popular theory is that the ghost is linked with either family members or domestic staff and an event or incident at St Margaret's House.

Lodge on Yarm Road, close to the junction with Butts Lane.

East window in St Mary's Church showing the Last Supper.

Visitations by a Former Landlord

For centuries – until Stockton's first road bridge was completed in the 1770s – Yarm Bridge was the lowest crossing point on the Tees and since the early 1800s it has been overlooked, on the northern bank, by the Blue Bell Inn.

There is a reminder of an earlier ill-fated bridge in the shape of a girder built into the ceiling of the Blue Bell. The single-span iron bridge collapsed into the river just before its official opening in 1806 and the old stone bridge was reprieved – and widened – to continue in use today.

The Blue Bell Inn is said to be haunted by a ghost of a previous landlord, George Goldie, who earned a reputation as one of the last salmon fishermen in the Yarm area. The Goldie family held salmon fishing rights along fourteen miles of the Tees for about 200 years, until pollution levels in the early 1920s made it unprofitable. George Goldie's reputation in the fishing fraternity was boosted still further on 3 June 1890, when he landed a 14½ stone Royal Sturgeon near Yarm. Measuring 8ft in length, and with a girth of 3ft 4in, it seems that it had moved upstream during a severe drought and was hauled in by Goldie at the confluence of the Tees and Leven.

The enormous fish drew thousands of admirers when it was put on show in the long room at the Blue Bell Inn. It was then displayed in a tent opposite Stockton Town Hall before being sold to a Newcastle based fishmonger. It is perhaps of no great surprise, then, that the spectre of George Goldie is said to frequent the various rooms and staircases of the Blue Bell Inn. During the mid-1970s, the incoming landlord decided to display a set of antique glasses on a solid glass shelf behind the bar. Standing about 5ft above floor level, it measured 6ft in length, 6in width and a quarter of an inch thick. The arrangement of glasses stayed in place for some two weeks, when, without warning and for no obvious reason, the shelf gave way. Although the shelf remained intact, every glass was shattered.

A couple of weeks later, the landlord got up during the night to visit the bathroom when he noticed the ghostly figure of a man on the landing. As he moved to investigate, the landlord walked through the apparition. Soon afterward, in conversation with the previous owners, it was agreed that the spectre exactly matched the profile of George Goldie.

Another strange episode was also linked to the ghostly presence of Mr Goldie. One evening, after closing time, staff members were enjoying a relaxing drink in the bar when water began to drip from the ceiling. Suspecting a leak from a pipe, the landlord raced upstairs and checked the whole area, but there was nothing to show. Returning to the bar, he found that a tea towel positioned directly below the dripping ceiling was wet but the ceiling itself had remained bone dry.

If further proof of a ghostly presence was needed, the reluctance of the landlord's dog to set foot in the cellar was noted as highly significant.

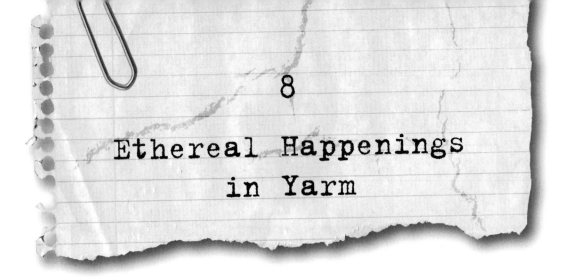

8

Ethereal Happenings in Yarm

THE original settlement of Yarm is set within a large loop of the Tees on the route of an old drove road through Yorkshire and northwards across the river into Durham. This strategic position may have attracted settlers in the pre-Norman period – the township's name is derived from the Old English 'gearum' meaning fish pools – and it seems that Yarm was noted for its salmon fishery in Anglo Saxon times.

By the second half of the twelfth century, a flourishing manorial borough was involved in shipping trade with Scotland, Flanders and France. A section of grey stone walling alongside the modern Leven Road is the only surviving masonry from the hospital of St Nicholas, established by Robert de Brus II in about 1130. The west end of the parish church is also said to date from the twelfth century and contains an unusual 'fish' window – an almond-shaped slot in the wall of the tower. Much of the church was rebuilt in the pseudo-classical style after a fire in 1728 and among features of interest within the building are the 'Moses Window', probably installed by William Peckitt in 1768, and an ornate Jacobean font.

Stone from the old hospital of St Nicholas was used to build Yarm's first grammar school, founded by Thomas Conyers on the south side of the churchyard in 1590.

For about 600 years between the twelfth and eighteenth centuries, Yarm was the major port on the Tees. Sailing ships ranging from sixty to 100 tons loaded exports of flour, wood, grain, hides, salt and lead at wharves that stretched from Silver Street downstream to the site of the skinnery on Atlas Wynd.

Merchants and traders had houses built on the High Street and the Dutch-style Town Hall, which was built in 1710, illustrates the links between Yarm and the Low Countries at that time. Pantile roofs are a feature of many buildings along the High Street, as pantiles were shipped into Yarm by vessels returning form Holland.

Flood levels of 1771 and 1881 are marked on the Town Hall and several of inns along the High Street have interesting associations. A group of local businessmen met in a room of the George and Dragon during February 1820 to plan a railway linking the Durham coalfields with the Tees at Stockton, while towards the northern end of the High Street Tom Brown's House – no longer an inn – is named after the local hero of the Battle of Dettingen in 1743, who charged into enemy ranks to recover the regimental standard. A memorial stone was unveiled in Yarm churchyard on 8 June 1969 by the Queen's Own Hussars, the modern counterpart of his regiment.

John Wesley is said to have visited Yarm on nineteen occasions between 1748 and 1788, and described the fascinating octagonal church of 1763 as 'by far the most elegant in England'. On the other side of the township stands Hope House, which dates from the early eighteenth century and is believed to be the oldest house in Yarm. A short distance away, along West Street, Yarm Castle sits proudly on the front wall of Commondale House. This cement model measures about 2ft in height and dates from 1882 when a local builder, David Doughty, created a number of items to decorate the gardens of this imposing redbrick property.

Yarm is dominated by a forty-three-arch railway viaduct, which carries the Leeds and Thirsk Railway from Northallerton to Stockton and Hartlepool. Construction work lasted from 1848 to 1852, with an army of navvies completing the forty-three arches that cover 760 yards.

During late October, Yarm's annual three-day fair takes place along the length of the High Street with gypsy caravans, roundabouts, sideshows and stalls bringing a special mix of noise, excitement and colour to cobbled areas on either side of the Town Hall.

With such a colourful and varied history stretching over many centuries, it should come as little surprise that several of Yarm's buildings have reports of supernatural visitations.

Ghostly Facets of the Friarage's History

In recent years, the Friarage has become the central building of a flourishing Yarm school complex. An earlier mansion dating from 1717 was remodelled in the early 1770s by Edward Meynell, with surrounding formal gardens, and this impressive property stands on the site of a Dominican Friary that was founded in about 1260 by the last Peter de Brus.

Following its closure in December 1539 the Priory was sold to John Sayer, Lord of the Manor of Worsall, and a room at first floor level in the rebuilt mansion was used as a chapel until the nearby Roman Catholic church was completed in 1860. Later owners include the Scrope family (1949-1954) and Head Wrightson & Co., who were based there for more than twenty years.

Down the years the Friarage has attracted reports of tunnels and subterranean rooms. Some of these secret passages were said to run for short distances to locations around Yarm and while remaining improbable, they have far more credibility than the fanciful talk of routes under the Tees to Egglescliffe parish church and many miles southwards to Mount Grace Priory.

The sense of mystery and intrigue around the the Friarage is increased by talk of ghostly figures. Some years ago, when the building was still in private hands, gardeners regularly reported seeing a monk in the grounds and there was also talk of a walking nun. In more recent times a spectral figure has been sighted on the top floor and a local resident with a house close to the Friarage reported that while sitting in his garden one evening, he witnessed a woman in medieval dress walk through his rear bedroom before disappearing into the perimeter wall.

Yarm's oldest inn, the Ketton Ox.

the Ketton Ox

Yarm's Oldest and Spookiest Pub – the Ketton Ox

Yarm is renowned for its range of hostelries offering food and drink to satisfy the needs of all age groups. Each building has its own particular history but the oldest and tallest of Yarm's High Street inns – the Ketton Ox – has had more than its fair share of haunting visitations.

The inn's exact age is unclear – with some estimates suggesting 400 to 450 years for this imposing building – but it was certainly named after a bull of huge size that was born at Ketton Hall, near Darlington in 1796. It served as a coaching inn when Yarm was still a major port on the Tees as well as an important market centre and, until about forty years ago, a central passageway ran through the centre of the inn to the stableyard at the rear.

Rumours of a tunnel running under the river remain unproven as the Ketton Ox's cellars have been filled in, but there is clear evidence of the blood sport of cockfighting in two rooms on the top floor of the building (and the rooms also included an escape shute for use when law officers raided).

Outhouses at the rear of the pub served for a time as the town's mortuary. These chequered episodes in the building's past may well be linked to a whole series of ghostly incidents.

Whilst sitting in the bar after closing time the landlord has, on several occasions, heard footsteps running across the living room on the floor above. His first thought, on each occasion, was that a customer had sneaked upstairs before he locked up, but the family dog was undisturbed and there was no human intruder to be found.

Looking northwards along with the Yarm High Street with Town Hall in the background.

At other times, the incredulous landlord watched his cigarette rock in the ashtray and then flip into the air before landing in the wastebin. Further strange occurrences include sightings of a ghostly eighteenth-century woman in a white cap and pale blue dress standing behind staff serving at the bar, and the cries of a baby during night time, when there was no young child in the building.

A Georgian Property with a Ghostly Presence

Yarm's prosperity as an inland port is shown by an imposing row of early Georgian merchants' houses at the southern end of Yarm High Street. Gardens stretch from the rear of these properties towards the riverbank, which were lined by wharves and warehouses.

For many years, the chimney and buildings of the Skinnery dominated on the upstream side and though they have now

The Keys, Yarm High Street.

been replaced by modern apartments, the splendid octagonal Methodist chapel (built 1763) continues in use on the other side.

John Wesley visited Yarm nineteen times between 1748 and 1788 and on

Cottages, former Methodist chapel
and windmill on Barwick Lane.

Former windmill on Barwick Lane.

each occasion, he stayed with George
Merryweather, a well-known merchant
and Methodist who lived on the High
Street. Early Methodist meetings were
held in a hayloft over the stables at the
rear of the house, before the chapel was
completed in 1763.

In recent years a resident in the
High Street property reported 'visits',
by a ghostly male figure dressed all in
black and wearing a tall hat. He had the
appearance of a Georgian clergyman or
preacher. Other members of the household saw him only rarely but reported
that the house seemed at times to have 'a
wall of coldness' and a young child was
moved into another room after seeing the
ghost appear through the bedroom wall.

Other people living there have heard
unexplained noises – usually banging or
thumping, and although the ghost was
generally regarded as an unpleasant char-

Georgian merchants' houses at the southern end of Yarm High Street.

acter, no one actually suffered any harm or serious upset.

Further personal investigation of the empty building identified, perhaps understandably, a rather cold and damp interior. Further detailed evidence came from previous residents. All the ghostly incidents had taken place at first floor level, in two rooms at the east end of the landing. Pet dogs were all very reluctant to venture past the doorway. One visitor, who was a scientist by profession, experienced a sudden feeling of coldness at the same location and also saw 'a group of (ghostly) people in the larger of the two rooms'.

Unnerving incidents at the Cross Keys Hotel

No doubt staff at Yarm's Cross Keys Hotel had plenty to chat about when they finally got the chance to take the weight off their feet after closing time. But, on occasions, their conversations were rudely interrupted by the sound of footsteps running across the floor above. Initially, the staff assumed that the noise it must be the landlord's young children chasing eachother around the bedrooms, but no they were not at home and there was nobody upstairs.

On another occasion, staff were sitting and chatting when a crashing sound was heard from behind the bar. Closer inspection showed that a cork from a bottle of cognac had shot out of the bottle and had smashed into optics.

The landlady reported a feeling of being cuddled when she was in bed, but she was alone. Surprisingly perhaps she did not find this incident unduly sinister – only unnerving.

At the end of the evening doors and windows were locked by staff. One window in the gents' toilet was usually left open during the course of the evening, so it was always securely locked after closing time.

One evening, whilst a barmaid was closing the window, all the toilet doors slammed shut. She turned to run out but the main door also swung shut and she wrenched at it in vain. Hearing her screams, her boyfriend pushed from the other side, only to find it open with ease …

Inexplicable activity continued in the main part of the pub, where a group of young men were drinking round a table close to the doorway to the gents. Suddenly, and without warning, a pint of lager rose from the tabletop and tipped over.

The incredulous men reported the incident to staff and then promptly left, never to return. As discussion continued among staff, there was talk of a playful poltergeist or the ghostly antics of a long dead drinker from the pub – who knows?

Unfriendly Figures at the Fellowship Hall

A series of rooms of different dates make up Yarm's Fellowship Hall on West Street.

The rear section was completed in 1822 and the main hall dates from 1897, while the middle part was probably included during 1838 as part of a chapel attached to the old school. A toilet block was opened in 1975.

The building was used as a Methodist chapel until 1932, and during the 1960s and 70s Yarm parish church held meetings on the premises before it was sold to Emmanuel Fellowship Church. In 1996, it was sold to Yarm Town Council and put to use as a community centre.

In recent years, a series of paranormal incidents have attracted the attention of ghost-hunting groups. Reports of spooky faces peering through the windows, shadowy figures around the building, anonymous voices and fleeting apparitions drew investigators to the West Street location. Within minutes of arriving in broad daylight, they became aware of the spirit of a little girl in the old part of the former church, but there were no clues to her identity...

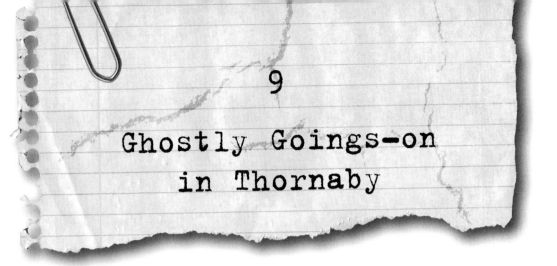

9

Ghostly Goings-on
in Thornaby

DURING the last two centuries, Thornaby has spread in both a northerly and southerly direction from the original settlement around St. Peter's Church, which still stands on the village green.

Thornaby is mentioned in the Domesday Book of 1086, though the church is not listed, but it was one of those given by Robert de Brus to the recently established priory at Guisborough during the twelfth century. After the Dissolution under Henry VIII's commissioners, ownership of Thornaby manor and church was removed from Guisborough Priory and between the sixteenth and eighteenth centuries, the church was a chapel of ease within Stainton parish.

Much of the existing building probably dates from the twelfth century and its most interesting internal feature is the chancel arch, which includes both Norman and Early English work. During 1970 the boundary hedge around the churchyard was removed to give all round views of the green.

Sundial House is located at the southern end of the village green and an inscription on the actual sundial includes the date '1621', indicating the building's original date of construction. Most of the properties

around the green date from the twentieth century but there is an atmosphere of timelessness around the little church, with ridges and hollows in the nearby turf providing interesting talking points.

During 1825, William Smith of Stockton opened a pottery works on riverside land about half a mile downstream from the village. Skilled workers were recruited Staffordshire and warehouses were opened in Rotterdam, Hamburg and Belgium as the brown pottery and ornamental items were exported from Thornaby. In 1838, further expansion took place close to the road bridge across the Tees as William Smith built workers' cottages and shops.

One of the north of England's first cotton mills was opened during the following year, and the new community of South Stockton expanded rapidly as timber yards, ship and boat-building yards and a general foundry were built within the curve of the river. By 1892, some 1,800 men were employed at the shipyards of Richardson Duck & Co. and Craig Taylor & Co. and in the same year, the redbrick Town Hall was opened at a cost of £7,000.

The focal point for this rapidly growing community was a large standard, which supported five gas lamps. Known locally as the 'Five Lamps', this distinctive structure included a drinking fountain and was the gift of three local magistrates. On 6 October 1892, the Municipal Borough of Thornaby was formed by amalgamating South Stockton and the old village of Thornaby, with a total population of 15,637. Poverty and hardship was particularly severe in Thornaby during periods of industrial depression, but a strong community spirit developed within this close-knit community along the southern bank of the Tees.

During the last forty years, there have been major changes in the Thornaby area. Land within the loop of the original river channel – Mandale Bottoms – formerly the site of Stockton racecourse, has been developed with a large shopping and leisure complex, while a sector of land close to Victoria Bridge has been redeveloped with housing, commercial premises and educational facilities.

In 1962, Thornaby Town Council acquired 347 acres of land adjacent to the former airfield and work got underway on a new town centre. The first stage of this development was completed in 1967 at a cost of approximately £4 million, and in the same year English Industrial Estate Corporation began work on an industrial estate for the Board of Trade. Since then, light industrial units have been developed on 350 acres of land, which was part of the former wartime airfield.

Opened in 1930, Thornaby was one of the first airfields to be set up after the First World War and it became an important Coastal Command base during the Second World War. During 1940, Hudsons of the 220 Squadron spotted the *Altmark* in Jossing Fjord and after a boarding party from HMS *Cossack* had transferred British prisoners to the allied vessels, Hudsons from Thornaby escorted ships back to England (and detected four floating mines in the convoy's path on the return journey).

Royal Air Force and Royal Canadian Air Force Squadrons flew Hurricane, Warwick and Spitfire aircraft from Thornaby in the later war years and in March 1944, it became an Air/Sea Rescue Training Unit, a role that continued for a number of post-war years.

The most dramatic reminder of Thornaby's aerodrome is a full-size replica Spitfire on the roundabout where Thornaby Road joins Trenchard Avenue. It was dedicated on 1 April 2007 and has markings showing the 608 Squadron's RAO and 401 Squadron Royal Canadian Air Force on either side of the fuselage. Another reminder of Thornaby aerodrome in the form of the Airman's Statue was unveiled on 8 May 1997 on a site close to Thornaby Road, and although some aspects of the airfield, such as runways and hangars, have disappeared in recent years, a number of buildings are still standing.

Peter – Thornaby's Ghostly Airman

The Station Headquarters, NAAFI building and Drill Hall are located in the Thornaby Road/Martinet Road area, and, during the early 1980s, the former RAF Officers' Mess became the focus for visitations by a ghostly airman. Thornaby Snooker Centre opened in the premises during October 1982 and there were soon reports of a sighting by a whole range of people associated with the building. 'Peter', as he soon became known, first appeared to a lighting contractor who was working in the club roof, and a few weeks later he made a more dramatic appearance. A cleaner who was working in the centre heard the loud clattering of balls coming from the snooker hall. On taking a look inside the room, she found that the tables were covered and all the balls safely locked up behind the bar.

Her first reaction was to attract the attention of a friend, but, as they made their way along the corridor, they were firmly stopped in their tracks by 'a loud noise like the sound of hundreds of hairdryers'.

Soon afterwards, other staffmembers at the premises had unscheduled meetings with Peter. Another cleaner felt a firm hand on his shoulder and also found that his bucket was repeatedly being moved. This led to talk of bringing in a medium to remove the ghostly presence, while contact with members of the Conservative Club that used to be based in the building merely confirmed the sightings.

With such a background of night flying, secret missions and countless stories of supreme bravery and personal sacrifice, it is perhaps not surprising that Thornaby, along with many other wartime aerodromes, has the spectral presence of an airman.

Ghostly Goings-On at The Griffin

In recent decades, much of the former airfield site at Thornaby has been developed with housing, schools, shops and other amenities, including public houses. During the late 1990s, The Griffin on Bader Avenue became the focus for a number of unexplained visitations by a gentleman in a long coat and trilby hat.

First seen by the landlord and his wife as they checked the premises after closing time, he went on to make several more appearances at this late hour. Discussions with dyed-in-the-wool drinkers at The Griffin indicated that this unexpected apparition closely matched the appearance of the pub's first landlord – an elderly gentleman who died on the premises of natural causes in the early 1970s.

On the first occasion, the landlord and his wife had closed the cellar door only for it to suddenly burst wide open again. Almost immediately, a wall of freezing cold air was transmitted from the cellar and, as

Old Thornaby Social Club.

they recalled, it was as if 'something invisible' was inside the cellar and determined not to be locked in.

Other strange episodes included light switches turned on and off by unseen hands, beer pumps inexplicably operating themselves and glasses flying off tables before smashing against walls, and, on a one-off occasion, a pint of beer anonymously appeared on a table – no one admitted putting it there and nobody dared touch it.

A spiritualist was brought in to check the premises and, without prompting, was able to confirm that a man in a long coat and trilby hat was present in The Griffin.

Unexplained Moving Objects and People

On some occasions, it is possible to explain the apparently illogical movement of household objects … but at other times it is certainly very difficult, if not impossible.

A former colleague of mine lived on the south side of Yarm between the A67 Thirsk Road and B1265 Worsall Road and often derived quiet amusement from watching guests' reaction when ornaments on the window ledge of his lounge shook and moved without prior warning and for no obvious reason. He had long since established that these apparently inexplicable movements were in fact the result of trains passing along the embankment behind the family home. Unseen and unheard, their weighty passage either to or from Yarm Viaduct was enough to trigger the temporary shaking motions that baffled guests until he enlightened them!

No such explanations could clarify incidents at Thornaby's Cobden Street a few years ago, when a row of ornaments that were placed in front of the living room fire were knocked over, during the night, on to the carpet.

Blame was apportioned to the family cat, but following other strange interludes there was talk of a resident spirit. The householders were in bed when a voice bellowed in the woman's ear 'Get out of my house!' and on another occasion the man of the house was alone in bed reading a newspaper when a faceless spectre made an appearance. Not surprisingly, the householder made a rapid exit from the property.

Discussion with the elderly lady next door led to her statement that she had seen the same vision walking through the wall of the terraced property.

Spectral Presence on Thornaby Green

There is a timeless air around Thornaby Green with curious grass-covered mounds and ridges spreading from Sundial Cottage, at the southern end, past the tiny church of St Peter ad Vincula towards Thornaby Low Wood and the banks of the Tees. Yet even this peaceful location has been the setting for reports of ghostly figures.

During 1974, a barmaid at Thornaby Village Club on the Green was making her way up the sloping roadway, opposite the club building, towards Thornaby Road when she spotted a tall figure wearing a long, black cloak and floppy hat. At his side was a black Labrador dog.

Taken aback by this strange sighting, the barmaid turned to point out the apparition to her friend but, much to her amazement, there was no one there. on turning back. Further enquiries among local residents provided reports of other sightings of this so-called 'Ghost of the Green'.

St Peter's Church on Thornaby Green.

Southern end of Thornaby Green, looking towards St Peter's Church.

The Griffin on Border Avenue, Thornaby.

Northern slopes of Thornaby Green, close to Thornaby Village Club.

St Paul's Church, Thornaby Road, built during the mid to late nineteenth century.

The Fox Covert, formerly the Half Moon, at High Leven on the A1044 Low Lane.

Ingleby Barwick's Ghostly Apparitions

The tract of land that spreads between the rivers Tees and Leven on the south side of Thornaby has seen phases of human occupation since the Bronze and Iron Ages, but in recent centuries much of the area has been farmland. From the late 1970s, however, work has continued on housing schemes that will result in a projected population of 25,000 by 2016.

A range of amenities has been completed including shops, schools and leisure facilities. It is at one of these – Bannatyne's Health Club on Myton Road – that staff have reported a series of unnerving supernatural incidents. Only on one occasion has

Bannatyne's Health Club, Myton Road, Ingleby Barwick.

Bannatyne's Health Club, Myton Road, Ingleby Barwick, - main entrance.

there been an apparition – a vague haze with no distinguishable features – accompanying the strange incidents but staff have given the supernatural presence the name of 'Olga'.

The health club opened its doors in 1998 and by the following year the unnerving episodes had begun …objects moving with no contact from human hands, lights flicked on and off and doors opening and closing by themselves.

Even more baffling were the showers, which had been checked at night to ensure that they had not been left on, were found the next morning to be on full blast.

In the kitchen area, staff watched in disbelief as utensils including knives and spoons were strewn around the room and on one occasion a jar of chutney projected itself through the open fridge door before smashing to the floor several feet away.

The only time there was any sort of apparition on the premises was when a member of staff came across a misty shape in one of the corridors. It had the vague outline of a human but slowly moved away through a solid wall, while the member of staff turned on her heel and ran.

Apart from this instance, all the other incidents seem to point to poltergeist activity and staff have come to regard these episodes with a degree of amused acceptance – rather like the antics of a wilful child who is repeatedly trying to test the adult's patience.

In looking for possible explanations, it has been pointed out that Bannatyne's Health Club covers ground that was at one time ancient woodland and an Iron Age settlement. During construction of a new roadway in the early weeks of 1997, an early burial ground was exposed and the suggestion has been made that Olga's grave may have been disturbed.

It happens in many urban settings, doesn't it? Large areas of housing means high numbers of commuters which inevitably, it seems, leads to serious rush hour traffic congestion.

Just a mile or two to the east, Middlesbrough has the so-called 'Marton Road Crawl', and with the spread of housing at Ingleby Barwick perhaps it was only a matter of time before there were similar build-ups in this area.

Much of the congestion centres around Thornaby Road (A1045) and the area of the Harold Wilson Recreation Centre and it is here that there have been reports, from motorists of 'highway apparitions'. A static, misty patch of air could be the result of tiredness or a puff of exhaust smoke, but no – a second concentrated look shows a roughly rectangular human outline with a smaller, child-like shape alongside.

Stuck in the line of stationary traffic, reports from motorists indicate that the baffling visions move and glide across the roadway before passing through the bonnet of the car to cross the kerb and grassy verge.

Clearance of housing and industrial sites means that traffic congestions is unlikely in Port Clarence on the northern bank of the Tees close to the Transporter Bridge. Yet even here, in normal traffic conditions, there have been reports of an apparition resembling a priest passing across the roadway in the vicinity of the site of St Thomas' Church. Dressed in old style clothing, the vision is said to have paused before passing through the bonnet of the car and then continuing across the road.

Durham Tees Valley Airport.

Hangars at Durham and Tees Valley Airport.

Series of Supernatural incidents at Durham Tees Valley Airport

In recent years the wartime setting of Goosepool aerodrome has been developed into Durham Tees Valley (formerly Teesside) Airport. It covers land close to Stockton's western boundary and though facilities were unfinished when war was declared in 1939, pilots of No.78 RAF Squadron were soon flying Whitleys against targets in Germany. No.76 Squadron flew Halifaxes from Middleton and both squadrons supplied over a score of aircraft for the first thousand bomber raids on Cologne.

The former aerodrome building – now International Fire Training Centre.

During the later war years, the Royal Canadian Air Force No.419 (Moose) Squadron occupied the station, flying first Halifax and later Lancaster aircraft against targets in France and Germany at a time when Middleton was the only bomber station north of the Tees.

Following the end of RAF operations at the base some buildings housed the Middleton St George College of Further Education, and the former Officers' Mess was converted into St George's Airport Hotel in time for the opening of the civil airport in 1966.

Reports of incidents associated with a ghostly airman began in the 1950s, when several flight crews described seeing the spectral 'flier' in hangars and hotel corridors. Successive reports continued when some of the buildings became a teacher training college, including mysterious and unexplained tapping on windows as well as footsteps on snow-covered areas that suddenly ended.

Most explanations for these strange episodes are linked to the heroic wartime actions of Canadian Flying Officer, J. McMullen, who was piloting a Lancaster bomber back to Middleton St George on 13 January 1945. His badly crippled aircraft was losing height as it headed for the aerodrome and, when it became obvious that it was not going to reach the base, he ordered the rest of his air crew to bale out while he stayed at the controls in order to crash land the aircraft away from built-up areas of Darlington. (McMullen Road in the town was named in his honour after the war.)

Other interpretations of these strange events suggest that the ghost is, in fact, another Canadian airman named Mynerski, who earned a posthumous Victoria Cross for his outstanding bravery when attempting to rescue a comrade from their blazing aircraft.

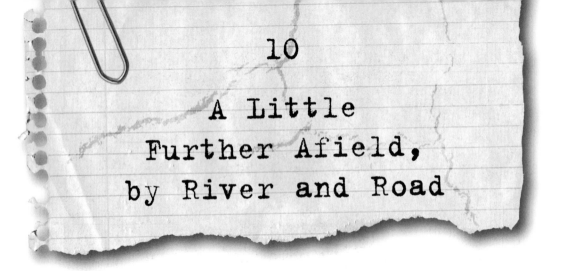

10

A Little Further Afield, by River and Road

DOWN the centuries the River Tees has played a major role in the development of townships such as Stockton, Thornaby and Yarm, and since the mid-nineteenth century heavy industry and more recently commercial and residential developments have spread along both downstream banks. Yet above Yarm and Egglescliffe, landscapes on either side of the river have remained largely unaltered.

Up and down the English countryside there are estimated to be 3,000 or more deserted medieval villages and several of these are located along this section of the Tees. Standing at these sites with faint outlines of trackways, the 'lumps and bumps' of people's houses it is all too easy to sense the presence of our early ancestors going about their day to day business.

The deserted village of Newsham overlooks the river between Low Middleton and Aislaby, It dates from the eleventh century and was made up of between eighteen and twenty-five dwellings in 1309, when the population probably stood at twenty. By 1390 one man owned the whole site, so it seems that the villagers were moved out at some point around this time.

Across the river, on the south side, many of High Worsall's secrets were uncovered during a *Time Team* investigation during October 1997. Above ground level the only remaining building is the ruined shell of St John's Church, which was reconstructed in 1719 with stone from an earlier church. It was last used on a regular basis in 1894 and by 1910 it served only as a mortuary chapel.

Detailed examination of the site unearthed further fascinating materials that pointed to a Roman presence long before the medieval villages occupied twenty long houses and a manor house complex. Written records highlighted some dramatic events at High Worsall including a murder in 1327, a visitation of the Black Death during 1349, robbery at one of the houses in 1351 and the conviction of eight men, including the chaplain, John Bull, for poaching fish from the Tees during 1362.

From 1354 the High Worsall estate was developed as a deer park by the Lord of the Manor, Thomas Seton, but there were still human visitors for many years afterwards as one of the later lords of the manor, or one of his guests, dropped a Henry VIII groat dating from 1544.

Mayor and Corporation of Thornaby-on-Tees, pictured in 1902.

Standing among the ruined walls of St John's Church as mist spreads from the nearby Tees, it takes little imagination to see a bustling community come to life.

Upstream from High Worsall and Newsham, the Tees begins a lengthy meander that encloses an even more dramatic setting at Sockburn. There is no remaining trace of the early village above ground level but experts believe that a major centre of Christianity flourished here before Viking raiders stamped their authority on the neighbourhood. A restored section of the church houses a fascinating collection of relics, including sections of stone crosses, medieval effigies and hogbacks.

One of the effigies is said to be that of Sir John Conyers, who is given credit for putting paid to the fearsome Sockburn Worm, whose final resting place is said to be marked by a large limestone boulder in a nearby field. The falchion or broadsword which was used to slay the 'worm' features in the ceremony on the nearby Croft Bridge when newly appointed Bishops of Durham are welcomed into the diocese.

There are several possible explanations for these monster legends (which are to be found in many parts of the country), including the presence of a large eel or river creature, but perhaps the most credible of these suggestions links the 'serpent' with an invading Viking army and a confrontation between the local hero and the enemy chieftain.

During my recent visit to this enthralling setting, a sudden roaring sound and turbulent movement of the waters in the Tees was soon explained by the sight of a farmer's track that had just crossed the river channel, but one is left wondering about secrets that await discovery as volunteers and experts continue work on the 'Sockburn Hall Project' – a long-term scheme to restore buildings and features on the site for residential or educational use.

Long before modern road systems crisscrossed the British countryside, travel was slow and fraught with danger. Between the mid-seventeenth century and the early nineteenth century, highwaymen were the scourge of anyone bold enough to venture on main routes such as the Great North Road or lonely roads and country lanes leading to towns and villages.

Best known of these villains is the infamous Dick Turpin – rather his greatest success was not as a highwayman, but as a cattle stealer, and he was hanged at York not for highway robbery, but for stealing a horse. Other highwaymen frequented routes in North Yorkshire and South Durham and the most notorious was probably Tom Hoggett.

His success at lifting purses over a wide area earned him a fearsome reputation. He was eventually captured by troops sent from York and held overnight under guard at the Salutation Inn, before being returned to York the following morning. The night was

Chapel housing effigies, hogbacks and sections of crosses at Sockburn.

Hogbacks and effigies in the chapel at Sockburn.

Greystone – according to local folklore the burial place of the Sockburn Worm.

Sockburn Hall, built in 1834.

stormy and moonless as Hoggett eluded his guards and made a dash for freedom in the hope of crossing the nearby River Swale at Langdon Ford, but in the darkness he stumbled into a pond and drowned.

Since then, on moonless and stormy nights, the ghostly outline of Tom Hoggett has been seen speeding on horseback along roads in the area. Without a hat, but with a caped coat reaching to his ankles and features highlighted by the flow from a lamp, Hoggett's ghost seems to be reliving his exploits.

Another notorious 'gentleman of the road' was William Nevison, who was imprisoned in York Castle. After bribing his guard, he escaped from captivity, but when King Charles II arranged a reward of £20 for his recapture, Nevison was soon caught and hanged on the Knavesmire at York. His ghost is said to haunt the roads that he terrorised in North Yorkshire.

Modern road systems hold no such fears for today's travellers, but there are still tales that defy rational explanation. A few years ago, a colleague in the teaching profession was driving back to Teesside with his family after a holiday in the south of England. As family members in the car slept soundly he drove northwards, mile after mile, in darkness and with little traffic on either side of the motorway.

After a while, he became aware of a single beam, presumably from another vehicle – perhaps a motorcycle – in his rear-view mirror. It did not come nearer – nor further away – but stayed behind at the same distance for many a mile. His wife was sleeping soundly in the passenger seat, while the children were slumbering peacefully on the back seat, so with no one with whom to converse, he turned into a petrol station. Surely, with this detour, the mystery light would disappear?

Back on the road, and still northbound, my colleague was dismayed to find that the beam of light was still firmly fixed in his rear-view mirror. It was the same distance behind and remained there for mile after mile as the family car headed homewards. Suddenly, there was an unexpected development.

Silently, and almost unnoticed, the beam moved steadily closer to the family car. Closer and closer it came until it was almost alongside, and then, without warning, and with no apparent side road to allow such a manoeuvre, the single beam of light swung to the right and disappeared from view. Inexplicably, the sinister light had gone and my colleague, with his unknowing family, was left to complete his journey back to Teesside.

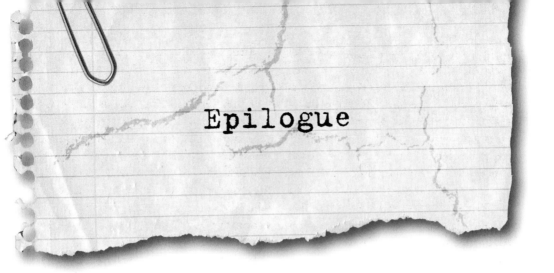

Epilogue

STRETCHING along both banks of the Tees, the current boundaries of Stockton enclose areas with a wealth of supernatural material from many different historical periods. Some reports are well substantiated, after thorough investigation, as I hope to have explored in this book, while other aspects are given only scant coverage with just limited basis in fact.

Given careful consideration, a number of cases can be readily assigned to the realms of folklore, while others may well be the product of an emotional state of mind at a time of crisis or tragedy; additionally, some undoubtedly result from perhaps the inebriated condition of spectators.

Enough incidents and examples remain to warrant serious consideration and possible explanation. Whether it is through participation in one of the many organised ghost walks in and around Stockton, or a serious investigative research project, there can be little doubt that the subject opens up a whole new perspective on areas of local life, which I hope you will enjoy investigating for yourselves, if you dare …

Index

Other titles published by The History Press

Durham Railways
CHARLIE EMETT

Ever since the Stockton & Darlington Railway opened in 1825 the north-east of England has been at the heart of the railway system. Charlie Emett, ex-railwayman, author and historian, has collected a fascinating selection of over 250 photographs, all informatively captioned. All County Durham's branch lines, past and present, are included in this pictorial guide, together with the East Coast main line, while the importance of Darlington's workshops and Shildon's wagon works is not forgotten.

978 0 7524 4955 5

Haunted Durham
DARREN W. RITSON

From Durham Castle to Jimmy Allen's public house, discover poltergeists, hooded apparitions, headless horses, phantoms, séances and exposed hoaxes. Containing many tales which have never before been published – including the crooked spectre of North Bailey and the ghost who bruised a barmaid's backside – this book will delight everyone interested in the paranormal.

978 0 7524 5410 8

The Coalminers of Durham
NORMAN EMERY

Coalmining in Durham was recorded as early as the twelfth century and medieval collieries flourished along the Wear Valley. The hardships and dangers of the miner's life are recalled in the pictures of the great pit disasters and the words of the survivors and rescuers, but the comradeship and community are never lost sight of and come into their own in the accounts of pit village life and of the famous Durham Miners' Gala

978 0 7524 5042 1

Tees Valley Curiosities
ROBERT WOODHOUSE

This collection brings together a series of unusual, intriguing and extraordinary buildings, structures and landscape features from across the Tess Valley. Included in these pages are fascinating relics from the area's industrial, ecclesistical and military past, including puzzling earthworks at Thornaby Green; Redcar's war-time early warning system; Yarm's octagonal Methodist chapel; and the intriguing primeval forests that lie off the beaches of Hartlepool and Redcar.

978 0 7509 5077 0

Visit our website and discover thousands of other History Press books.
www.thehistorypress.co.uk